Gourmet Camping

A Menu Cookbook and Travel Guide for Campers,
Canoeists, Cyclists, and Skiers

Gourmet Camping

A Menu Cookbook and Travel Guide
for Campers, Canoeists,
Cyclists, and Skiers

by
Joan Wilcox Osborne

Illustrated by Gail P. Kohl

QUAIL RIDGE PRESS
Brandon, Mississippi

DEDICATION

To Mom whose love means taking care and
To Dad whose love means freedom to ramble.

Library of Congress Catalog Card Number: 87-90827

Library of Congress Cataloging-in-Publication Data

Osborne, Joan Wilcox.
Gourmet camping.

Includes index.
1. Outdoor cookery. I. Title.
TX823.O73 1988   641.5'78   88-18271
ISBN 0-937552-23-2

Color cover photo courtesy David Trufant.
Cover black and white photo courtesy U.S. Forest Service.
Cover design by Barney McKee.

Contents

Contents

6

Acknowledgments

There is no way to thank everyone who contributed to the ideas that resulted in this book, but I'll start with the River Rats who were running delicious camping trips when I was just imagining them; most especially to my first sternman, Mike Osborne, and to Johanna Huber, Hulin Robert, Carol Clark, Caroline Dott, Betty Wood, Jerri Hanemann, Frances Bendana, Susie Fox, Christie Johnston, Charlie Fryling, Jessie Metevier, Denise Stigge, Carol Anderson, and Margie McInnis, who generously shared their camp cooking secrets. And also to Tuffy Clark, Doris Falkenheiner, Harry Stille, Jean and the late J.P. Wiggin and John, Sissy, Mark and Charlie; to Janet and Earl Higgins, Lois and Rick Norton, Bob Blair, Orlando Bendana, Pete Hanemann, Leonard Huber, Vernon Wright, Oliver Houck, Bryan McDaniel, Bill Heath, Merrill Stigge, Tom Kambur, Bob McComiskey, Ben Brown, Ed Knox, Donald Wood, Julie and Bill Penick, Anne and Don Bradburn, and so many more who shared the good times and a few hair-raising ones as well.

Without the help of Wayne Richardson-Harp, who patiently schooled me on backroads bicycling; Mary and Frank Chaffin, Nancy Kirk, Sara Murphy, and Aurelia Kennedy, who offered editorial and moral support; Patricia and Dick Watson who loaned not only encourgement but a word processor; and Caroline Loupe and Glenn Turner who made Maine possible, this book would still be a mass of good intentions. My editor, Gwen McKee, applied her abundant energy and her good, clear mind to the task of producing a much more reliable and useful book than I was heading for, and Gail Kohl further enhanced it with her imaginative drawings.

My family gave enormous help. Colleen Carpenter tested recipes through a long, hot summer. Pat Wilcox shared her knowledge of Napa Valley wines; Laurie Wilcox-Meyer and John Meyer shared their condo and their spirit of adventure, as did John Wilcox who taught me to catch choupique and rescue cows. Jim Wilcox proved the method works by overcoming a camping phobia left over from eating raw bacon on a Boy Scout survival trip in 1961. My son Johnny and daughter Caroline were always a joy to camp with and still are. And my husband, Tim Fields, was the one person who was sure this book would finally get written. And because of that, it did.

Author Joan Osborne, formerly of Mandeville, Louisiana, paddling the swamp in her own backyard.

Introduction

This is a book for people who love thundering whitewater, thrumming river swamps, Gulf dunes, piney campgrounds, and snowy mountain trails; especially if they also love a fine camp dinner of Chicken Sauce Piquant and Chocolate-Glazed Carrot Cake. I wrote this book to share two ideas: (1) camp food can and should be just as adventurous and pleasurable as camping itself, and (2) great camp food can also be easy on the cook. These simple, but rather startling ideas emerge in accounts of camping trips my family and friends have taken across the Southeast and beyond—and in the descriptions of mouth-watering meals that made each trip memorable.

I've spent much of the past 18 years camping. On mountainsides and riverbanks, in campgrounds and under bridges, I've hung out with some of the best camp cooks around. With their help, I've developed a method of turning out fresh and original camp food that still leaves plenty of time to climb bluffs, identify asters, and snooze under a sycamore—all the things we go camping to do. The secret is advance preparation of certain special dishes, combined with an array of easy-to-assemble menus full of the fresh fruits, vegetables, and specialties of the season.

For a long time I've been itching to talk back to outdoor writers who relegate camp cooking to a single juiceless book chapter or admonish in magazine articles that "the use of dried, canned, and dehydrated food is mandatory." So often their message, explicitly or implicitly, has been that camping and comfort don't mix. And folks, it just ain't so. Camping is probably the most comfortable, rewarding, and totally sensuous pastime I know. Well, almost. But you'd surely never know it from reading recipes combining canned beans, canned macaroni and cheese, and chopped bologna into grim combos called "Camper's Stew" or "Gunny Sack Goulash."

Thankfully, not all camp cookbooks have been quite so spartan. Recent books suggest a new approach, implying at the very least that camp cooks should be trying harder. But how hard? One recipe from a widely available book lists 15 separate ingredients to be toted to camp for a "made-from-scratch" beef stew. That stew further requires the cook's crouching attendance over the camp stove for a good part of the afternoon...not my idea of a peak camping experience. Another of the "try-hard" books raised some Cajun eyebrows when it specified a can of onions as an ingredient in chicken gumbo. People who know gumbo would no sooner add dead onions to roux than they'd marinate live gold-fish for seviche. To put it gently, many recent camp cookbooks appear to have been written by folks who know a lot more about camping than they do about food.

I have been lucky to live in Louisiana, a state where both the outdoors and food are taken seriously. Buoyed by our philosophy of *laissez les bon temps rouler*, we Louisianians take a camping trip as we take a holiday—both are occasions to celebrate! Consequently, we almost always eat better in camp than we do at home. And why not? Good food makes good trips better and bad trips bearable.

Take for example the Thanksgiving our group of camping River Rats caravaned northeast to the Great Smoky Mountain National Park to celebrate the holiday Cajun style and "let the good times roll." With our four camp stoves hissing as one, we cooked up such a feast—marinated shrimp, smoked turkey, and all—that half the campers at Elkmont were on hand trying to seduce the cooks into dinner invitations. Other times, comforting food was the only thing left when all else had failed, as it most certainly had one rainy November night in the middle of a frog-cold Atchafalaya Swamp. This trip, ironically, had been billed as an entertainment for paying guests, though after an all-day down-pour, the entertainment level had sunk lower than a snake's belly. All 16 guests were scrunched under a dripping tarp on a shrinking island of gumbo mud, chilled to the bone and totally dispirited. It wasn't until my partner and I produced a steaming pot of wine-laced cassoulet and double helpings of warm pecan pie that our clients were restored, if only temporarily, to life and hope. Nothing else short of a helicopter ride home could have done as much.

My belief in adventurous camp cooking is inextricably linked to a belief in equal rights for camp cooks. As far as I'm concerned, few camp meals should take more than a half-hour's time to serve forth. The pages that follow will show you how, for they're full of fresh ideas for make-ahead camp food, dishes ideal for camp but rarely served there—things like Tony's Creole Stuffed Pork Roast, Gumbo Z'herbes, and Strawberry Fool. *At Home, To Pack,* and *In Camp* instructions for each dish make the cook's job even easier since most of the work is done before you ever set foot in camp.

As you know if you've done it, planning a weekend's worth of

Introduction

camp meals at a crack takes no time only if you always serve the same old thing—peanut butter lunches, hot dog dinners, and instant oatmeal for breakfast—and lots of folks do. But how dull. In this book you're served up whole meals of delicious camp food—exciting ideas for all kinds of trips from spring beach camping to a couple's winter getaway, from a lakeside celebration of the Fourth, to a fall color whitewater trip. All the work of harmonizing meals with each other; with the camping, canoeing, or loafing motif of the trip; and with the bounty of the seasons, has been done for you. Planning great meals will take you no time at all, and I dare you to find a single dull one in the bunch.

Even so, this book probably isn't for everyone. There will still be campers like the ruthlessly permed lady I met in an Everglades campground who told me she fed her husband varying species of the same genus of canned soup nightly in the Winnebago "because we had to leave the microwave in Orlando." And then, I hope, there is you, the adventurer: you who value a cold night, a high white moon, your companions around the campfire and your food and drink with equal enthusiasm. You're not afraid to try something different—whether it's swamp canoeing or catfish courtbouillon—just for the fun of it! I hope the pages to come will take you places you want to go.

Before We Begin: What a camp cook should know that a home cook may not.

1. Fight Entropy. Entropy is the tendency of the best-laid camping plans to gradually fall apart under the pressure of drizzle, malaise, or a small inner voice nagging you to stay home and rake leaves. Adventurous campers go, no matter what, since rain clears the air, malaise evaporates outdoors, and the leaves will wait.

2. Fight Inertia. Inertia is the tendency of bodies (yours) cooking chicken spaghetti to keep right on cooking it trip after

Introduction

11

trip. Resist the temptation to repeat camping menus, even successful ones. Tackle something new on every trip, try every recipe in this book (they're all good), then hitch up your belt and go looking for more.

3. Make Lists. I don't care who you are and how much your mind resembles the proverbial steel trap, write it down. Be warned by what I ("an experienced camper") forgot: (a) the coffee—on a bone-freezing morning in a windswept camp: (b) the cooking pots—they waited in the driveway while the chicken simmered in beer cans by the fire: (c) the wine—not just any wine, the Chianti Classico for a gilt-edged spaghetti dinner that wasn't quite the same with root beer: (d) a complete fish dinner—actually the fish, etc., inadvertently left in the trunk of a shuttle car which is why we were still frying them at 10:30 p.m. Don't smile. Sooner or later you will come up with something just as gauche...unless you write it down. (And sometimes even then you'll forget.)

Joan's spring vegetable/herb garden.

4. Keep It Simple. Smaller trips are simpler trips; our maximum is usually no more than six to eight adults. Don't worry about kids; they're easier to manage in camp than anywhere else, as long as you bring more than one.

5. Buy Quality. Great cooks are great shoppers first, and know where to find ripe cheeses, fresh yard eggs, locally-grown vegetables, and sweet-smelling fruit. They don't buy wilted "fresh" broccoli just "because it is there." Quality comes easier if you have a small garden plot, nothing fancy, with room enough for green onions, parsley, mint, basil, and lettuce, at least.

6. Buy Adventurously. Do you realize most people probably buy little more than 100 different food items, year in and year out? Step out of that rut to sample some of the thousands of interesting doodads most of us are too insecure or too lazy to try: chopped liver, Feta cheese, pesto sauce, Italian biscotti cookies. You won't believe what you've been missing!

7. Serve the Right Food at the Right Time. Spaghetti and meatballs on a summer beach? Not in my lifetime. In hot weather, campers droop and drink a lot, but shrink from heavy food, so serve plenty of unsugary liquids and light, spicy entrees—things like shrimp-pasta salad or antipasto platters.

In winter it's just the opposite. Cold weather campers eat three huge meals a day, cookies in-between, and crave the dread duo, meats and sweets. Metabolizing protein produces extra warmth, and sweets answer our body's call for quickly metabolized fuel, so our cravings even make sense physiologically. All in all, winter camping is a great time to indulge in an occasional orgy of eating. I've seen many a vegetarian if not exactly fall off the wagon, at least eye our pork roast with pained nostalgia. And no one ever said no to the pineapple pie.

On strenuous trips——any day you'll be burning calories on the water or trail—— make it an inviolable rule to eat a power-packed breakfast and lunch. Bitter experience speaks; memory of the time the River Rats impulsively opted to run Section III of the Chattooga River, a last-minute decision that put us in such a frenzied time crunch, we barely had time to gulp down a slice or two of charred breakfast toast. The ensuing seven-hour paddle was so exhilarating we postponed lunch till 2:00, but so exhausting it left us as depleted as salmon after the spawning and at dusk barely able to hang on to the paddles. We finally finished the last quarter mile (including a fierce portage around Bull Sluice) in darkness so total we navigated solely by touch and by the sound of roaring water. We survived, but we were dumb. Two good meals on time would have made all the difference.

8. Keep It Flexible. Inviting folks camping isn't the same as inviting them to dinner; somehow camping trips are always in flux. Manage it by packing food in small containers so that if half your group cancels out, leftovers can remain or return home. Too much food is better than not enough; one black night you just might find yourself stranded on that riverbank with a few unplanned meals in the offing. I've been looking forward to it for years.

9. Take It Easy. To avoid last-minute panic, prepare your camp meals well in advance. Shop early. Cook and bake freezable dishes ahead of time. Then, once you have planned, bought, cooked, and packed for a trip, enjoy it. Mealtimes should find you seated in a camp chair, ankles crossed, sipping your coffee or wine, and giving orders to the team. And remember: the camp cook does not wash dishes.

10. Maximize Your Effort. Many of the recipes you'll cook or bake for a camp meal can be doubled and half the food frozen for another day. Great camp cooking pays dividends even after the trip itself is over.

11. Share the Load. The last but most important rule of all: don't go it alone! The menus to come are simple enough for a moderately experienced cook or careful beginner to prepare with ease. Therefore, unless you have an Escoffier-complex, why do it all yourself? Simply assign each family member or camping friend a meal or part of a meal to cook and serve. If two families camp together, the Kirks bring breakfast, the Haymakers bring dinner, and each brings lunch and drinks to share. You'll find that virtually everyone, spurred by friendly rivalry, rises nobly to the challenge and the resulting meals rise from obscurity to compliments.

Packing It Up

The best camp cooks abhor clutter: too much equipment complicates their job. You will save yourself money, time, and a cartload of frustration if you stick to the best equipment, and not much of it. Before you buy, study camping magazines and camping equipment catalogs, then compare the prices, quality, and service of camping stores, hardware stores, and mail order houses. The prices especially may surprise you.

My interest in and knowledge of equipment is rather casual; I know what works for me and that is what I'll pass on. Here is the equipment I have found necessary and desirable (not always the same thing):

Necessary Equipment:

1. Camp Stove. After experimenting with eight models, from a three-burner Coleman to a single-burner Svea, I'm still seeking the ideal stove. Easy to use, safe, powerful, economical, quiet, lightweight, durable, cheerful, brave, thrifty, reverent, and roomy enough for two big pots—I can't seem to have it all. At least not in one stove. Therefore I, like most camp cooks I know, have two: a single-burner for summer trips, long distance traveling, or backup; and a big powerful two-burner for everything else. Because I am slow mechanically, I prefer a propane cylinder stove, a snap to operate. On the downside, its disposable propane cylinders aren't cheap and need replacement every few trips. Coleman-type stoves, those using white gas, are a little crankier, but less expensive to operate, and most of my friends think they're fine.

2. Pots. In choosing pots, you need to strike a balance between weight and durability. Lightweight is better as long as it doesn't depend on inferior materials. Steer clear of cheap aluminum, the very worst cooking material imaginable. My choice is a nested set of rounded (for easy cleaning) stainless steel or high quality aluminum camping pots with covers and broad folding handles. The capacity of the largest pot is 1 1/2 gallons, so the set easily handles most of the cooking needs of eight or fewer. The pots cook and warm food, boil water, hold salads and desserts, even act as a double boiler to warm rolls. The tops double as plates or platters. A canvas drawstring bag just for pots is a boon to organization.

Your kitchen pots can pinch hit for a while in camp, but if you do much camping, you'll soon realize the physical and psychological advantages of having a complete camp kitchen ready to roll.

3. Steamer. A roomy stainless steel or enamel steamer does a major job that nothing else does so well: it heats foil-wrapped food or breads. As you'll discover, many of the recipes that follow call for a steamer.

4. Non-stick 10-inch Skillet. Use the skillet mostly for frying or scrambling eggs or for two-camper cooking. A folding handle is important.

5. Lightweight Pizza Pans or Trays. No, not for pizza, but for anything needing room: fresh fruits or vegetables, summer

cold plates, appetizers, or bread to be sliced. Two aren't too many and they pack easily in the bottom of a duffle.

6. Plastic Plates, Insulated Plastic Cups. Look for a material like Lexan, durable and lightweight. Insulated cups are important, preferably calibrated for use as measuring cups. Label plates and cups with names of camping regulars so owners can find, wash, and put away their own. Chasing dinnerware is not the cook's job.

7. Lightweight Cutlery. Knife-fork-spoon sets are sold on rings or in plastic cases for organized types. We keep a varied selection of cutlery in coffee cans, and transport what we need in the potholder mitt along with utensils.

8. Utensils:

Knife. A medium-length, thin-bladed sharp knife in a sheath will do for vegetables, meats, and breads.

Spatula. Protocol requires a plastic or wooden spatula for the non-stick skillet, though I prefer to tear up the skillet rather than the eggs with a short-handled metal spatula (when I remember it). Once we flipped pancakes with a piece of cardboard...not recommended.

Wooden Spoons. For stirring food as it cooks; they're lightweight and won't burn the hand that stirs.

Ladle. For serving stews and soups and such, Sierra cups work well and save space. As far as I'm concerned, this is their highest calling outside backpacking.

Can Opener. One that opens bottles, too.

Tongs. With reach and efficiency, you can lift hot corn, steak, foil packages, or serve almost anything.

Corkscrew. Unless you like straining cork fragments through your teeth.

9. Potholder Mitt. Also a handy traveling case for cutlery and utensils.

10. Salt and Pepper Shakers. Small plastic shakers with flip-top covers; fill salt shaker half full of rice to absorb moisture, and keep them both covered.

11. Food Containers. Most often I transport cooked food, frozen or unfrozen, in Ziploc freezer bags. They maximize ice chest space and can be refilled with leftovers or tossed out when empty. We always travel with spares. Some food needs more protection than a flexible bag provides; for things like cooked pork chops that may fragment, use a plastic container with a very tight press-on top. I have occasionally used widemouth screw-top plastic jars for stews and such, although cleaning plastic in

Introduction

camp is never fun. A neat idea, especially for long trips where you have several frozen entrees, is a Dazey Seal-A-Meal which lets you seal food in boilable plastic bags and heat and serve it right from the bag. For coldweather lunches, a half-gallon thermal jug holds hot stew or soup (Gott makes one with a 6-year warranty).   Lighter weight Ziploc bags carry salad fixings, cheese, or other non-messy food, and for salad dressings, sauces, and other messy things, I use sturdy throwaway glass jars. For sandwich mayonnaise and mustard, save the bright yellow mustard squeeze containers and label one "Mayo."

12. Beverage Containers. A sturdy stainless steel quart thermos is a godsend on cold mornings; pouring hot coffee right into a thermos from the pot keeps it hot without further attention. Have you ever slept with a thermos? Stow it in your sleeping bag and drink hot or at least very warm coffee the next morning without leaving the tent—a peak experience.

For tea, coffee, milk, juice, and *vin ordinaire*, I use quart glass or plastic juice containers or half-gallon plastic milk jugs. The aforementioned half-gallon thermal jug holds iced drinks in summer. A gallon milk jug almost filled with water and frozen serves double duty in the ice chest providing both cooling power and drinking water. Add a few lemon slices for flavor.

13. Ice Chest. You will likely need at least one large and one medium ice chest or cooler. Of the several I have owned, Igloo and Coleman performed well. We took two Igloos full of block and dry ice down the Colorado River in August, and ended the 10-day run with the only cold beer on the raft. Gott features refreeze bottles inside the lid of their model which makes sense since cold air sinks and cools on the way down. Block ice lasts much longer than cubes. Make your own in pots, half-gallon milk containers, or plastic bottles, and enjoy the extra ice water as it melts in the bottle.

Keep your ice chest protected from the sun with a wet towel or boat cushion, shade it when you can, and open it 50% less than you do now. A smaller chest is a handy container for bread, cookies, and other crushable items as well as lunch plates and utensils. Keep Igloos and other such coolers away from fires; they burn explosively.

14. Tarp. Your camp kitchen must be roofed if rain is remotely possible. (In Louisiana this is 98.6% of the time.) You can make no better investment than a large (12x12-foot or more—more is best) lightweight nylon tarp. Though not cheap, they can transform a rainy trip from a disaster into a party.

Introduction

15. Waterproof Matches and Fire Starter. Carry matches and fire starter cubes or ribbon in a medium-sized widemouth plastic jar. Stash another small metal container of matches in the pot bag for emergencies. Bring lots of matches for stove and campfire and test them regularly to make sure they're still alive. Waiting on a wet beach with a skillet of raw pork chops and a box of damp Victorias, praying for a canoe to happen by with a spare kitchen match is too cruel a price to pay for memory lapse...take it from me.

16. Water Jugs. Plastic gallon milk jugs make fine inexpensive water jugs. Water containers larger than a gallon I find hard to wield. One gallon per person per weekend is usually adequate for cooking and drinking, if you have other beverages along.

17. Heavy Duty Aluminum Foil. Always handy for covering pots or wrapping bread or rolls for warming. Carry a generous quantity of folded or rolled-up foil in the pot bag.

18. Detergent, Scrubber, Bleach. A small flip-top plastic bottle of detergent, a non-rusting copper scrubber, and a small plastic bottle of bleach to sanitize dishwater or deodorize after seafood make up KP supplies.

19. Paper Towels. You can't live without paper towels in camp. Use them for scraping and washing dishes and pots, for drying things, for wiping sand off things, and of course for emergency toilet paper.

20. Heavy Duty Plastic Lawn and Leaf Bags. Portable garbage bags for every speck of your trash, plastic bags can also waterproof your gear or you in a sudden shower. A clean bag, flattened, makes a small but necessary work surface if you lack a table, pad, or groundcloth.

21. Ziploc Freezer Bags. Extra bags for leftovers or for collecting wild foods like chanterelle mushrooms in July, pokeweed in March, or blackberries in May.

Desirable Equipment:

1. Coffeepot. Since I usually bring pre-made coffee from home, on short trips this is used mainly to boil water for tea. On long trips, it's essential and it's also handy for the dark and deadly Cafe Brulot.

2. Cake Tin. A metal tin (a very large cookie tin) holds not only cake, but pies, muffins, or rolls, and allows for gentle warming by the fire.

3. Griddle. A must for pancakes, as far as I'm concerned, since even with my lightweight but stickless griddle, I must tussle

with pancakes to get them just right. Also good for cooking lots of fried eggs or burgers or grilled sandwiches.

4. Lightweight Grill. For campfire-grilled meats, kebabs, or emergency cooking if the stove has the vapors.

5. Pot Drainer. Looks like a big, slotted knife; a help in draining pasta, vegetables, or rice. Hulin the Great drained pasta without one one dark night and was mighty grateful for the dark as he scooped errant fettuccini out of the bushes with his bare hands.

6. Miniature Whisk. More efficient than a fork for whipping cream, something we seem to do a lot of in our camp.

7. Paper Plates. If I were more environmentally sound, I'd tell you not to use them, but sometimes they do come in handy. Mostly for greasy or tomatoey food that takes forever to remove from plastic plates.

8. Plastic Wine Glasses. Not for every trip, only for uncommon celebrations like Mardi Gras in Mississippi.

9. Candle Lantern. An inexpensive, romantic light. If you plan to play poker or perform surgery, bring a Coleman.

10. Onion Sacks. For large group trips, grocery stores are happy to provide mesh sacks for canned food and for such hardy fruits and vegetables as grapefruit, oranges, lemons, pineapple, cabbage, potatoes, and, yes, onions.

11. Folding Table. Camp cooking can murder your back; not only that, the tough guys are always kicking sand in the Dirty Rice. With a folding aluminum or vinyl table, your aching erec-

tor spinae and sand won't be half the problem. Without a table, we make do on regular trips with a groundcloth or four-foot folding vinyl-covered pad which my daughter previously used for nursery school naps. On canoe trips, sometimes we up-end a boat for a table, but they're tippier upside down, so brace them sturdily.

Whipping Your Gear Into Shape

We now have a jumble of equipment in need of an organizing principle; here is my suggestion:

1. Label everything. With a waterproof permanent marker, write your name on all the gear you own; on big items like the ice chest, include an address and phone. This not only saves you pawing through three red Igloos on a group trip, but may also facilitate return of strays. Label small items with colored tape or pick a repugnant pattern for your cutlery—anything to make sure all your gear follows you home.

2. Make a home place for your gear. Big enough, visible enough, so that everything you use is in clear view. A basement wall of shelves is ideal. Or move out of your bedroom. But make room!

3. Organize your gear according to function. Stove stuff—propane canisters, fuel bottles, matches—all goes in one place. Keep it there always and forever. When you stow your gear, stow it clean or leave it out until it gets clean. If it is broken, get it fixed.

4. Choose a travel container for each functional set of gear. Orange canvas bag: stove, fuel bottle, matches. Always. Knowing what is in a bag just by looking at it cuts down on fumbling, the curse of camp-pitching. It also streamlines your packing since after a while you won't have to think about where you pack what.

5. Keep essential gear ready to roll. Some gear stays packed. In my tough-as-nails green duffle goes salt and pepper, Ziploced paper towels, tea bags, plastic bags, and other essentials. When it's time to go, I just add the plates, cups, cutlery, and utensils we'll need along with the sturdy food items that finish off that bag. If you use a large kitchen bag as I do, it helps to group like items in smaller plastic bags inside, and don't forget the waterproofing.

6. Pack from a list. Check off gear as it comes off the shelf. Make a list of every item to pack into each ice chest or dry food

container, and don't leave till each item is checked into its container. Otherwise stated: pack in haste, repent at leisure.

Taking Care

Just a word on taking care of the outdoors before we set off to take it on:

1. When you leave a campsite, clean it just as thoroughly as you clean your own house when company's coming...because it is.

2. Don't be too proud or too lazy to pick up other folks' trash. Maybe your example will keep others from perpetuating the vicious cycle of littering.

3. Be scrupulously careful about campfires. Bury them and douse them until they're dead out. I scoffed until I almost set a pine tree aflame with five minutes of inattention.

4. Wash dishes in a big pot of warmed soapy water away from streams or lakes; it's easier and you won't pollute even a little bit.

5. Treat landowners with respect; never camp on posted land and always leave their land better than you found it. Maybe that way they'll all come around to welcoming campers instead of praying we don't show up.

About the Book

The pages that follow are filled with revelry, in the accounts of twenty-seven celebrations of our camping seasons in the wild. The menus are power-packed and adventurous, just as we were at the time we ate them. And each meal is suited to the place, the action, and the season of the year. So now if you're ready, let's go gourmet camping!

Introduction

Spring

Paddling beneath the majestic cliffs that rise above Arkansas' Buffalo River.

1

Up and Running With the Buffalo: An Ozark Whitewater Canoe Trip

All winter, canoeists within driving distance of northern Arkansas dream of a spring run down the Buffalo National River, a paradise of bluegreen pools, sun-spattered willow runs, and streaked bluffs so daunting that paddlers camping ant-like below can't help feeling just slightly irrelevant.

When the water is up and running after a spring rain, the 23.5 fast-water miles between Ponca and Pruitt challenge and delight us paddlers from the flatlands, although if you're not pure extrovert, you'd best launch on weekdays or afternoons to avoid bank-to-bank paddlers jostling for river room. Let the crowds go by and give the Buffalo all the time it deserves: take the time to explore caves and crannies, climb bluffs, trek to Hidden Hollow (a surprise waiting for you to happen), and don't forget to bring along food worthy of one of the grandest rivers in the South.

For information on the Buffalo River:

Ozark Society, Inc.
P. O. Box 2914
Little Rock, AR 72670

Excellent reprints and books from the *Ozark Society Bulletin* provide information on streams, trails, and natural history.

Lost Valley Canoe & Lodging
Buffalo National River
Ponca, AR 72670
501/861-5522 or 5523

Canoe and raft rentals, shuttles, river information, guides, mountain cabins, bunkhouse, and store.

Buffalo National River
P. O. Box 1173
Harrison, AR 72602-1173

Map list, including USGS; canoeing guides for sale, as well as free items including Buffalo River newsletter, *Currents*.

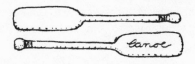

MENUS
(* indicates recipes given)

Breakfast

Cranberry Juice
Breakfast Steaks in Butter* • Cheese Bread* • Fig Preserves
Celestial Seasonings Morning Thunder Tea
Chocolate Milk for Kids

Lunch

Jip's Salmon Salad Sandwiches* • Frozen Pickles*
Small Sweet Oranges • Ginger Ale

Dinner

Smoked Almonds • Ozark Spring Salad*
Chicken Sauce Piquant*
Boiled Rice*
Chocolate-Glazed Carrot Cakes*
Wine: A spunky red such as Louis M. Martini Barbera
Milk for Kids

Breakfast Steaks in Butter

6 small steaks (round,   1 stick butter
   sirloin tip, or tenderized)   Salt and pepper

At Home: Freeze steaks in Ziploc freezer bag

To Pack: Steaks, 1 stick butter, salt and pepper.

In Camp: Heat butter in skillet or on griddle. Pan-fry thawed
steaks over high heat until browned on each side and done to your
specifications. Season to taste. Serves 6.

Cheese Bread

This bread also makes fine toast, fried on a lightly-buttered skillet or griddle.

1 1/4 cups milk
1 tablespoon sugar
1 teaspoon salt
1/2 tablespoon butter
1/2 package dry yeast

1 tablespoon lukewarm water
2 3/4 cups all-purpose flour
1 1/2 cups shredded sharp
   Cheddar cheese
Melted butter

At Home: Grease medium loaf pan. Scald milk, add sugar, salt, and 1/2 tablespoon butter and cool till lukewarm. Soften yeast in water and add to cooled milk mixture. Add 2 cups flour and mix well; add cheese and remaining flour and mix again. Knead dough on floured board for 5 minutes or until smooth. Place dough in greased bowl, brush with melted butter, cover, and let rise in warm place until double.

   Knead dough and shape into loaf. Place in loaf pan, brush with melted butter, and let rise until even with top of pan. Preheat oven to 375 degrees.

   Bake for 30 minutes or until bread is golden and emits a hollow sound when thumped. Remove from pan, cool, wrap in heavy foil, and freeze, if you like.

To Pack: Bread, butter, fig preserves.

In Camp: Heat wrapped bread in steamer over tea water, turning frequently to insure even heating. Serve warm with butter and fig preserves. Makes one medium loaf.

Jip's Salmon Salad Sandwiches

My brother Jip, who writes novels as James Wilcox, invented these sandwiches in his 36th year and shocked the family. We were under the impression his sole culinary talent was eating.

1 (7 3/4-ounce) can salmon,
3 tablespoons minced celery
2 tablespoons minced onion
3 hard-boiled eggs, finely
   chopped

1 tablespoon lemon juice
1/3 cup mayonnaise
Pepper to taste
Whole wheat bread
Leaf lettuce

At Home: Mix flaked salmon with celery, onion, eggs, lemon juice, mayonnaise, and pepper. Keep very cold and transport to camp in small plastic container or jar.

To Pack: Salmon, whole wheat bread, mayonnaise, Frozen Pickles, leaf lettuce.

In Camp: Serve on mayonnaise-spread whole wheat bread with Frozen Pickles and leaf lettuce. *Variation:* Add 2 tablespoons chopped green stuffed olives to mixture and omit pickles when making sandwiches. Makes about 8 sandwiches.

Frozen Pickles

These are the easiest pickles you'll ever make, delicious either as pickles or as tangy-sweet side dish.

1 pound unwaxed cucumbers
   (4 cups, packed), sliced thin
3/4 pound yellow onions
   (2 cups, packed), sliced thin
4 teaspoons salt

2 tablespoons water
1 cup sugar
1/2 cup cider vinegar
1 teaspoon dried dill or
   a sprig of fresh dill

At Home: Mix cucumbers, onions, salt, and water in a large bowl and let stand 2 hours. Drain.

Return vegetables to bowl; add sugar, vinegar, and dill. Let stand, stirring from time to time, until sugar dissolves and liquid covers vegetables. Pack in Ziploc freezer bags and freeze.

To Pack: Pickles.

In Camp: Serve thawed, but ice-cold. Makes 1 quart.

Ozark Spring Salad

Violets and redbud trees bloom abundantly in the April Ozarks and make delightful additions to a salad.

Leaf lettuce
Redbud flowers

Violet flowers and tender
leaves

DRESSING

1/4 cup olive oil
1/4 cup raspberry vinegar

1 teaspoon sugar
Salt and pepper

At Home: Mix olive oil, vinegar, sugar, salt and pepper to taste in a small jar. Pack washed lettuce in Ziploc bag.

To Pack: Dressing, lettuce.

In Camp: Search for tender violet flowers, light green violet leaves, and redbud flowers. Toss greens and flowers with dressing.

Boiled Rice

At Home: Measure rice, one-third as much dry as you want cooked, and transport in Ziploc freezer bag. About 2 1/2 cups raw rice is sufficient for 6 ravenous campers.

To Pack: Rice, water, salt, pot drainer, steamer.

In Camp: In bottom of large steamer pot, bring salted water to boil. Add rice, stir, and boil uncovered until just tender. Drain rice into steamer section and let it sit over barely simmering water to steam dry and fluffy. *Note:* If you're really in a hurry, you can cook your rice at home, transport it in a Ziploc bag, and reheat in the steamer. You can even freeze cooked rice (with some loss of vigor.)

Chicken Sauce Piquant

A favorite South Louisiana recipe, hot and spicy, whose dark brown roux is the soul of the dish. It is also wonderful, with buttered spaghetti.

6 tablespoons oil
6 tablespoons all-purpose flour
1 1/2 teaspoons salt
2 teaspoons pepper
1 teaspoon white pepper
1/4 teaspoon cayenne
1 teaspoon garlic powder
1 teaspoon thyme
6 pounds chicken pieces, washed and dried (skinning is optional)
3 green onions, chopped
2 stalks celery, chopped
1 large onion, chopped

1 medium green pepper, chopped
3 large cloves garlic, minced
1 tablespoon jalapeno peppers, chopped
1 (1-pound) can tomatoes, cut up
1 (1-pound) can tomato sauce
2 bay leaves
1 tablespoon Worcestershire sauce
1 cup water (or 1/2 cup water and 1/2 cup red wine)
1/2 pound sliced mushrooms

At Home: In large iron pot, mix oil and flour and cook over medium heat until mixture is a dark chocolate brown roux.

Sprinkle chicken with salt, peppers, garlic powder, and thyme, and brown it in the roux. When brown, remove chicken and add green onion, celery, onion, green pepper and garlic, and cook for 5 minutes.

Add jalapeno peppers, tomatoes, tomato sauce, bay leaves, Worcestershire sauce, water or wine, and mushrooms, and simmer for 30 minutes. Return chicken to pot, correct seasonings (it should be hot!) and simmer until chicken is tender. To save space you may want to bone the chicken. Transport refrigerated or frozen in Ziploc freezer bags or plastic container.

To Pack: Chicken Sauce Piquant, Sierra cup.

In Camp: Heat piping hot and serve over Boiled Rice. A Sierra cup makes a handy ladle for pot dishes of this kind. Serves 8-10.

Chocolate-Glazed Carrot Cakes

A nutritious dessert that tastes too good to be health food, freezes well, and keeps unfrozen for a week.

1 1/4 cups boiling water
1 cup oatmeal, uncooked
1/2 cup margarine
1 cup sugar
1 cup packed brown sugar
2 eggs
1 teaspoon vanilla

2 1/4 cups all-purpose flour
1 1/2 teaspoons cinnamon
1 teaspoon baking soda
2 cups shredded carrots
3/4 cup raisins
1 cup chopped pecans or
   walnuts

At Home: Butter a 15x11x2-inch rectangular cake pan. Preheat oven to 350 degrees. In small bowl, pour boiling water over oatmeal, cover, and let stand 15 minutes.

In large bowl, cream margarine, sugar, and brown sugar until light; blend in eggs and vanilla, and add oatmeal.

In small bowl, sift flour, cinnamon, and baking soda, and add to oatmeal mixture. Mix well. Stir in carrots, raisins, and nuts. Pour in prepared pan. Bake at 350 degrees for 20-25 minutes or until cake tests done. Let cool.

CHOCOLATE GLAZE

2 squares unsweetened baking
   chocolate
3 tablespoons butter
3 tablespoons heavy cream

1 1/2 cups sifted confectioner's
   sugar
1/2 teaspoon vanilla

At Home: Melt chocolate and butter over low heat. Stir in cream and then confectioner's sugar, and mix thoroughly. Cook over low heat, stirring constantly, for about 3 minutes or until starchy taste disappears. (Always cook confectioner's sugar frostings briefly for this reason.) Add vanilla and blend.

Ice cake while glaze is still warm. Once cake has cooled, cut into rectangles, wrap in waxed paper, and transport in cake tin. Keep cake cool.

To Pack: Just the cake.

In Camp: Enjoy! Makes 15 generous servings.

2

Spring at Santa Rosa:
Beach Camping in Florida

On Santa Rosa Island, easternmost of an island chain happily preserved as the Gulf Islands National Seashore, our U.S. Park Service has hidden away a surprise: a peaceful, private group camp. With enough polite letters and perhaps a phone call or two, you may be lucky enough to reserve it for your special group.

Go in May before summer's full heat, and pitch your tents in the shade of pines blowing with sea wind. Get up early and chase sandpipers; scavenge the Pensacola docks for wholesalers of blue crabs, red snapper, and white or brown shrimp; swim with the dolphins in bathtub-clear water; and relax right down to your bones.

The beach food we brought and bought—light, plentiful, and foolishly easy to serve—left plenty of time for naps and laps and sand dollar hunts.

For information on Santa Rosa Island:

Superintendent, Gulf Islands
  National Seashore
P. O. Box 100
Gulf Breeze, FL 32561-0100
904/932-5302

Florida Campground Assn.
1638 North Plaza Drive
Tallahassee, FL 32308-5323
904/656-8878

Camping, group camping, touring Fort Pickens, bicycling.

Campground registration
904/932-5018 (days)

Send for Florida Camping Directory (free of charge)

Sea oats anchor the dunes of Santa Rosa.

Breakfast

Alabama Banana Bread* • Homemade Sausage Patties*
Cantaloupe Halves with Vanilla Yogurt
Coffee • Chocolate Milk

Lunch

Greek Salad* • Crusty Rolls
Green Grapes • Green Apples • Butter Cookies
Limeade*

Dinner

Pickled Okra • Radishes • Celery Sticks
Pepper Cheese Sticks
Santa Rosa Boiled Shrimp and Sauce*
Potent Potato Salad* • Strawberries Devonshire*
Dixie Beer • Root Beer for Kids

Alabama Banana Bread

Dense, rich and banana-y, this loaf is delicious warm or cold for breakfast, lunch, or tea. Keeps well, too.

1/2 cup margarine	3/4 teaspoon baking soda
1 cup sugar	1 teaspoon baking powder
1 egg	1/2 teaspoon salt
1 1/2 cups sifted, all-purpose flour	3 large ripe bananas, mashed
	3/4 cup pecans, chopped

At Home: Grease and sugar loaf pan; preheat oven to 350 degrees. Cream margarine and sugar till light; beat in egg. Blend in sifted dry ingredients and mashed bananas, then add pecans, and pour into loaf pan. Bake at 350 degrees until bread tests done with clean straw, about 50-60 minutes. Do not overbake. When cool, remove from pan and wrap in heavy foil. Freeze, if you like.

To Pack: Banana bread and butter.

In Camp: Heat foil-wrapped bread in top of steamer over coffee-water and serve thinly-sliced plain or with butter. Serves 8-12.

Spring / Spring at Santa Rosa

Homemade Sausage Patties

Want to escape nitrites, nitrates, and glutamates? Try this.

1 pound ground pork	1 teaspoon pepper or to taste
1 pound lean ground beef	1/2 cup beef stock
1/2 teaspoon garlic powder	1/4 cup dried milk powder
1/4 teaspoon allspice	1 teaspoon jalapeno pepper,
1/4 teaspoon nutmeg	minced or
1/4 teaspoon ginger	1 teaspoon hot pepper
1 teaspoon paprika	flakes or to taste
1 teaspoon salt or to taste	1/2 teaspoon liquid smoke

At Home: Mix ingredients. Cook a small amount and test for seasoning. Form into patties and wrap separately in plastic wrap. Freeze in Ziploc freezer bags.

To Pack: Sausage patties.

In Camp: Fry patties in skillet or on griddle until browned and cooked through. Grilled over coals, these patties make a savory supper dish on a short backpacking trip. Makes about 36 patties.

Courtesy of Florida News Bureau Department of Commerce.

Florida's Panhandle...where silver sand meets blue-green water.

Greek Salad

Refreshing. Try a sandwich made of the oil-drenched tomato and Feta on a crusty roll.

1 head iceberg lettuce, torn
1 head curly endive, torn
1 large green pepper, in rings
16 Kalamata (Greek black) olives
6 anchovy fillets, drained and rinsed

3 green onions, chopped
3/4 pound Feta cheese
1 pound fresh green beans, cooked tender-crisp
3 ripe tomatoes
6 sprigs parsley

At Home: Wash vegetables and pack in Ziploc plastic bags; cook beans. Mix the following ingredients in small jar:

DRESSING

1/2 cup olive oil
Juice of 2 medium lemons
1 clove garlic, minced

1 teaspoon oregano
Salt and freshly-ground pepper to taste

To Pack: Lettuce, endive, and parsley, pepper and onions, olives, anchovies, cheese, tomatoes, beans, dressing.

In Camp: Arrange lettuce, endive, green pepper, green onions, olives, anchovies, and green beans in large bowl or on platter. Crumble Feta cheese over top. Garnish with tomatoes cut in wedges and parsley sprigs. Shake dressing and pour over salad. Serves 4-5.

Butter Cookies

Buy a good brand such as Pepperidge Farm, or make your own. In summer, buy.

Limeade

5 large juicy limes
1/2 cup sugar

1/2 teaspoon grated lime peel
Water to make 1 quart

At Home: Juice 4 1/2 limes. Mix lime juice, sugar, lime peel, and water to make 1 quart. Slice 1/2 lime and add to mixture. Transport to camp in plastic bottle or pitcher.

To Pack: Limeade

In Camp: Serve over ice garnished with lime slices. Serves 4 once.

Santa Rosa Boiled Shrimp and Sauce

Any seafood brought to camp from home must be resoundingly fresh and stored on ice in its own ice chest; otherwise, buy it from a source near camp. "Resoundingly fresh" means virtually without odor except for a faint ocean tang.

1 bag crab boil	6 quarts water
1/2 cup salt	4 pounds fresh headless
2 lemons, cut up	shrimp

SAUCE

1 1/2 cups catsup	3 tablespoons prepared
Juice of 2 lemons	horseradish or to taste
Tabasco to taste	

At Home: Mix sauce ingredients and transport in jar.

To Pack: Shrimp, crab boil, salt, lemons, water, covered pot, sauce, plastic bags, newspapers, clean-up jar.

In Camp: Combine crab boil, salt, lemons, and water in large covered pot. Bring to boil and boil 5 minutes before adding shrimp. When water returns to boil, cook shrimp for 4 minutes if they are smallish and 6 if they are large. Do not overcook. They should be firm, almost crisp. Drain immediately and serve hot with sauce. Makes 6-8 servings.

Clean-up note: Cover the table or eating area with newspapers, bring heavy plastic bags and dilute bleach solution in a jar for clean-up, so that next day camp won't smell like low tide at high noon.

Spring / Spring at Santa Rosa

Potent Potato Salad

Unlike timid modern versions with their white wine and their teaspoonful of chives, this potato salad has oomph.

8 medium red potatoes,
  boiled just tender,
  then peeled and diced
5 hard-boiled eggs,
  chopped coarsely
4 green onions, minced
1 large garlic pickle,
  chopped fine
2 tablespoons pickle juice

2 stalks celery, chopped fine
10 radishes, sliced thin
1/2 cup salad olives, chopped
1 cup mayonnaise
  (or enough to moisten)
3 tablespoons prepared yellow
  mustard
Salt and pepper, particularly
  pepper, to taste

At Home: Mix potatoes, eggs, green onions, pickle and juice, celery, radishes, and olives. Add mayonnaise and mustard while potatoes are still warm. Season with salt and pepper, and toss gently. Transport in wide-mouth plastic jar or bowl and keep very cold.

To Pack: Potato Salad, extra mayonnaise.

In Camp: Fluff it up with a bit more mayonnaise, if necessary. Makes 8-10 generous servings.

Strawberries Devonshire

This ultra-simple, impressive dessert is nice for brunch, too.

2 (3-ounce) packages
  cream cheese
1 1/3 cups heavy cream

2 pints strawberries
Brown sugar

At Home: With electric mixer, whip cream cheese until soft and fluffy. Beat in cream until blended. Transport to camp in wide-mouth jar.

To Pack: Strawberries, cream, brown sugar.

In Camp: Wash and hull berries. Spoon cream mixture over berries and sprinkle with brown sugar. Makes 6-8 servings.

3

Discovering Beaver Creek:
An Exploratory Canoe Trip

Spring, a green avalanche rolling through the Louisiana winter, brings leafy woods, luminous blue skies, and, for house-bound campers, a sometimes dangerous urge to explore the unknown. One day it brought us to Beaver Creek.

Beaver Creek hadn't looked like much on the map, just a tiny line squiggling into a bigger one labeled "Amite River," but with

Courtesy US Forest Service (Mississippi).

Secret beaches invite discovery.

April buzzing outside, we were ready to transcend maps and uncertainty, and so we arrived on a creek bank where no one had gone before.

There we found a storybook stream, miniature, but perfectly navigable, where sparkling water ran beneath canopies of oak, blackberries hung heavy and thick in the sun, and hidden beaches invited a picnic at every bend. Paddling Beaver Creek was an idyll, justifying in a day so many exploratory trips where our enthusiasm ran aground on low water, blind alleys, or fallen trees. Nevertheless, when you go exploring, it's wise to bring comforting food...just in case.

There are no directions to this place...it's mine! Anyway, the point of exploring is to find your own. Happy hunting.

MENUS
(*indicates recipes given)

Breakfast
Orange-Mint Sierra Cups*
Pineapple Muffins*
Soft-Scrambled Eggs*
Lapsang Souchong Tea*

Lunch
Wild Turkey Sandwiches*
Yogurt with Sliced Nectarines
Iced Tea with Mint

Dinner
Birdseed*
Orange-Glazed Pork Chops* • Margurite's Stuffed Potatoes*
Green Salad with Herb Dressing*
Blackberry Pudding*
Wine: A full-bodied white such as
Round Hill Chardonnay

Orange Mint Sierra Cups

Sweet seedless oranges   Mint leaves

At Home and To Pack: Oranges and washed mint leaves.

In Camp: Peel and section the oranges and serve in Sierra cups garnished with fresh mint leaves. And by the way, if you don't grow mint, you're missing a small but significant pleasure.

Pineapple Muffins

Make a double batch and freeze half for a lazy Sunday morning at home.

1 (20-ounce) can crushed pineapple, drained (reserve syrup)
1/2 cup sliced almonds
2 cups all-purpose flour
1 teaspoon baking soda

1 (3-ounce) package cream cheese, softened
1 cup sugar
2 teaspoon vanilla
1 large egg, beaten
1/2 cup sour cream

GLAZE

1 tablespoon margarine or butter
2 tablespoons pineapple syrup

1 cup confectioner's sugar, sifted

At Home: Heavily butter 24 muffin pans or 48 tiny muffin pans and sprinkle with almonds. Preheat oven to 350 degrees. Sift flour with baking soda. Beat cream cheese, sugar, and vanilla till smooth; blend in egg. Add flour mixture alternately with sour cream. Fold in drained pineapple. Spoon into muffin pans and bake at 350 degrees until muffins are delicately browned, about 25-30 minutes (less for tiny muffins). Remove from oven and let stand 5 minutes. In small pan, mix Glaze ingredients and cook briefly over low heat until starchy taste is gone. Spread glaze on muffins. When cool, remove muffins from pan and store in cake box or Ziploc freezer bags. Freeze, if you like. Makes 24 (48 tiny) muffins.

To Pack: Muffins, butter, foil, steamer.

In Camp: Wrap in foil and heat in top of steamer. Serve with or without butter.

Soft-Scrambled Eggs

1 tablespoon butter
16 fresh eggs
1 cup whipping cream

Salt and pepper
Minced chives or green onion
 tops

At Home: To save space, break eggs into a jar and keep cold.

To Pack: Eggs, butter, cream, salt and pepper, chives or green onion tops.

In Camp: Mix eggs and cream till just blended. Start eggs in a barely heated skillet filmed with melted butter. Keep heat low and stir infrequently. When eggs are just set, add salt, pepper, and a stingy shower of chives or green onion tops. Serves 8-10.

Lapsang Souchong Tea

The smoky distinction of this classic tea is just right with the sweet muffins. It is fine for winter trips, too, when a hot tea and cookie break is not only esthetic, but occasionally life-saving.

Wild Turkey Sandwiches

Thin-sliced turkey breast
 (home-roasted, I hope)
Thin-sliced jalapeno cheese
Mild onion

Tomato
Avocado, ripe and soft
Outer leaves of romaine
Crunchy bran bread

At Home and To Pack: Prepare and pack turkey breast and cheese. Bring along onion, tomato, avocado, romaine, bread, and a tray.

In Camp: Thinly slice onion and tomato, mash avocado into a soft butter. Place on platter along with other ingredients. Spread bread with avocado butter and layer with other ingredients as you like.

Spring / Discovering Beaver Creek

Birdseed

My buddy Ed Knox's special favorite (when he can't find a steak).

Almonds	Sunflower seeds
Cashews	Celery salt
Walnuts	Cayenne
Pecans	Onion powder
Soy nuts	Soy sauce
Sesame seeds	Oil

At Home: Mix ingredients, adding seasoning to taste and soy sauce and oil just to film nuts. Spread in roasting pan; roast in 350-degree oven, stirring frequently till toasted, about 20 minutes. Do not burn!

To Pack: Birdseed.

In Camp: Pass it around with such potables as you enjoy.

Orange-Glazed Pork Chops

An easy, lush dish that pairs well with lightly-cooked green beans or broccoli.

4 center-cut, 3/4-inch pork chops	2 cloves garlic, minced
1 (6-ounce) can frozen orange juice concentrate	Tiny pinch rosemary
2 cans water	1/8 teaspoon thyme
	Salt, pepper, and cayenne to taste

At Home: Brown chops, using their own trimmed fat to grease pan. Arrange in skillet in single layer. Dilute orange juice with 2 cans water, pour over chops, and sprinkle them with garlic, herbs and seasoning. Cover and simmer until chops are tender, checking sauce level and adding more orange juice if necessary. When tender, uncover and correct sauce consistency. You should aim for a creamy consistency sufficient in quantity to spoon over chops. Transport chops and sauce in plastic container.

To Pack: Pork chops, orange.

In Camp: Heat chops in sauce and serve garnished with orange slices. Makes 4 servings.

Margurite's Stuffed Potatoes

These are irresistible, so count on two halves per person.

8 medium Idaho potatoes
1 stick butter or margarine
1/2 cup milk
3 green onions, minced

1 cup grated sharp Cheddar
 cheese
Salt, pepper, cayenne to taste

At Home: Bake potatoes until soft. Cut in half lengthwise, and scoop out centers, leaving a 1/4-inch shell. With electric mixer, whip potatoes, butter, and milk until fluffy, adding more milk, if necessary. Mix in green onion and cheese, and season to taste with salt, pepper, and cayenne. Stuff mixture into shells and bake at 325 degrees for 10 minutes. Wrap potatoes individually in heavy foil and freeze, if you like.

To Pack: Stuffed potatoes, butter, tongs, steamer.

In Camp: Heat foil-wrapped potatoes in top of steamer. Serve in foil topped with butter. Makes 8 servings.

Green Salad with Herb Dressing

1 pound fresh spinach,
   washed, dried, and trimmed
Inner leaves of 1 head romaine

Small mild purple onion
2 hard-boiled eggs, sliced

DRESSING

6 ounces olive oil
2 ounces red wine vinegar
1 teaspoon salt
1/4 teaspoon freshly-ground
   pepper

1/4 total cup chopped fresh
   herbs: parsley, chives,
   chervil, tarragon, savory,
   and basil

At Home: Wash and dry greens, and store in Ziploc bag. Mix dressing ingredients and transport in jar.

To Pack: Greens, purple onion, 2 hard-boiled eggs, dressing, tongs.

In Camp: Toss greens and onion rings with dressing. Garnish with sliced eggs. Serves 6-8.

Blackberry Pudding

2 cups blackberries
1 1/2 cups water
2 1/2 tablespoons cornstarch
3 tablespoons cold water

1/4 cup sugar
1 cup heavy cream, whipped
Extra sugar

To Pack: Above ingredients separately; or berry mixture, whipping cream, and sugar.

At Home or In Camp: Simmer berries with 1 1/2 cups water for 10 minutes. Mix cornstarch with 3 tablespoons cold water, and add to berries; simmer 5 minutes more. Add sugar and refrigerate. Transport in plastic container. Serve in a cup, alternating berry mixture and whipped cream. Top with sugar.

When you whip cream in camp, be sure to have a miniature whisk or fork, a small metal round-bottomed pot, and the heavy cream—chilled. Then pass the bowl among prospective diners, so all hands can whip up on the cream. Makes 6 servings.

4

Country Roads:
Backroads Bicycling in Louisiana

Once you've tasted the freedom and exhilaration of backroads bicycling, you'll revel in the miles and miles of country roads waiting to be explored. Whether you'll revel in camping at the end of those miles is another question, one I frequently answer "no."

I discovered this weakness on my first bicycling trip when I, an over-30 friend, and 12 teenagers took off from my cabin on the Amite River to burn up the backroads of neighboring Ascension and Iberville Parishes. For most of the long, sweaty, happy day crisscrossing the fragrant countryside on bumpy asphalt roads, I managed to keep up. We tooled along past golden sheets of butterweed, live oaks and cabins, soybean fields and country stores, and stopped only when our enormous Cajun breakfast wore off (in my case about 10:00 a.m.) for a plain, but good biker's lunch. All day long pushing it—but game—I kept up.

Only when the sun dropped low and we geared down the driveway into the yard where the kids and ostensibly we adults would be camping, did I rebel. Two of us ended the day indoors with showers, candlelight, Johannisberg Reisling, roast chicken, and no apologies. Reveling in bicycling and recovering indoors made an excellent combination that day, and still does on occasion.

For information on bicycling in Louisiana and elsewhere:

Louisiana Department of
   Transportation
P. O. Box 44245
Baton Rouge, LA 70804
504/342-7849

Parish (county) maps are a boon to backroads bicyclists.

...necca for backroads cyclists: the country store.

MENUS
(*indicates recipes given)

Breakfast

Strawberries in Orange Juice*
Fried Eggs with Cheese and Herbs*
Go-For-It Grits* • Grilled Andouille*
Cafe au Lait*

Lunch

Edam Cheese • Granny Smith Apples
Macadamia Nuts • Bittersweet Chocolate
Water with Lemon Slice

Dinner

Red and White Radishes • Green Onions
Herb-Roasted Chicken* • Spring Peas*
Homemade White Bread*
Strawberry Fool*
Wine: A delicate white such as the reasonably priced
Firestone Johannisberg Riesling

Strawberries in Orange Juice

Strawberries   Fresh orange juice

At Home or In Camp: Place washed, hulled berries in small glass
(at home) or cup (in camp) and cover with fresh orange juice.

Fried Eggs with Cheese and Herbs

An offering from the beneficent Reverend Glenn Turner.

Pinch garlic powder	2 tablespoons butter
Pinch marjoram	6 large fresh eggs
2 tablespoons snipped parsley	2 tablespoons water
6 tablespoons grated cheese,	Salt and pepper to taste
Cheddar or Jack	

At Home or In Camp: In small bowl combine seasonings and cheese. Heat iron skillet over medium heat for 2 minutes, add butter and break in eggs. Immediately sprinkle eggs with seasonings and cheese and add 2 tablespoons water. Cover tightly. Count three and turn off heat. Eggs will cook in steam in three or four minutes. Serve with Go-For-It Grits, butter, salt and pepper to taste. Makes 6 servings.

To Pack: All separately; or seasonings and cheese mixture, butter, eggs, salt, pepper, water, iron skillet with cover, spatula.

A word on the importance of the hard-to-find fresh egg. Seen one lately? You really can't fry a stale egg; instead, you'll end up with a downtrodden sort of pancake. So locate fresh eggs even if it means a weekly drive across the Mississippi River Bridge, as it does for me.

Go-For-It Grits

5 cups water   1 cup grits (not instant)
1 teaspoon salt

At Home or In Camp: Bring salted water to boil, slowly stir in grits and return to boil. Reduce heat and cover. Cook gently for ten or more minutes, stirring occasionally. For cheese grits, add 1 cup shredded sharp cheese at end of cooking. Serves 6-8.

To Pack: Grits and salt premeasured in Ziploc bag, measuring cup, water, and cheese.

Grilled Andouille

Andouille is a plump garlic sausage, a specialty of Acadian Louisiana, and if you can't buy it locally, come down to LaPlace, Louisiana, and get some. It's best split lengthwise and cooked for 10 minutes in simmering water to cover, then drained and grilled in a hot iron skillet until crisp and brown. Two pounds will serve 6-8.

To Pack: Andouille, iron skillet.

Spring / Country Roads

49

Cafe au Lait

6-8 cups hot dark roast coffee   1/3 cup cream
3 cups milk

At Home: Make your coffee as usual but stronger, and chill the resulting extract in a plastic or glass bottle. Carry to camp in the ice chest.

To Pack: Coffee, water, milk, cream, and sugar, thermos to hold hot coffee.

In Camp: Heat coffee with extra water and the milk and cream, bringing it just to a simmer. Proportions are about half coffee, half creamy milk. Purists will heat milk and coffee separately and pour in cup simultaneously. Sugar is optional. Makes 6-8 servings plus refills.

Cheese and Apple Lunch

Quality is the difference between a forgettable or an unforgettable lunch, *especially* when meals are simple, as this one is; buy the best—a genuine Holland Edam, crunchy apples, exotic nuts, the best chocolate, and fill your water bottle with lemon-flavored ice water, partially frozen to start off.

Herb-Roasted Chicken

A classic roast chicken in the French style.

1 plump (4-pound) chicken   1 sprig chervil or 1/2
1 large clove garlic   teaspoon dried
2 tablespoons butter   1/2 cup green onion tops,
2 cups chicken stock   snipped
Juice of 1 lemon   Salt and pepper
1/2 cup parsley, snipped

At Home: Preheat oven to 450 degrees. Wash and dry chicken and rub inside and out with cut clove garlic and 2 tablespoons soft butter. Pour stock and lemon juice over chicken. Stuff half the herbs inside chicken and rub the remaining herbs under and over skin. Tie wings and legs close to body with soft string.

Roast chicken on its side on a rack in a shallow pan. After 10 minutes turn chicken on other side. Brush with butter and roast for another 10 minutes. Reduce heat to 350 degrees, turn chicken on back, brush with butter, and roast for 1 hour, basting every 10 minutes with butter or pan juices. After 50 minutes, test chicken for doneness by piercing thigh with a fork. If juices run clear, chicken is done. Remove chicken from oven, salt and pepper to taste, and wrap in heavy foil or put in plastic container. Serves 3-4 (or 2 with leftovers for lunch).

To Pack: Chicken and parsley.

In Camp: Remove string and garnish chicken with parsley. Serve air temperature or heated in foil wrappings in steamer.

    Variation: Roast small squab chickens or Cornish hens. Save leftovers for chicken sandwiches with Sesame Mayonnaise.

Spring Peas

1 cup water

2 pounds fresh green
  peas shelled (or
  2 [10-ounce]
packages frozen peas)

1 tablespoon sugar

2 tablespoons butter

1/4 cup heavy cream

Salt and pepper to taste

To Pack: Peas.

In Camp: Serve very hot.

Homemade White Bread

This sounds like trouble and is the first few times, but the bread you get for your pains is more than worth it. Note: Health food store baking yeast gives best results.

4 cups milk, scalded	1 package dry yeast
1/4 cup sugar	1/4 cup lukewarm water
4 teaspoons salt	12 cups sifted bread flour
2 tablespoons shortening	Soft butter

At Home: Grease three loaf pans. Add sugar, salt and shortening to scalded milk and let cool till lukewarm. Soften yeast in 1/4 cup water and add to cooled milk.

Stir in flour gradually, mixing slowly and thoroughly—eventually, use your floured hands. Knead on floured board until smooth and satiny, about 8 minutes, adding flour if dough is sticky. Shape dough in ball, place in greased bowl and rotate dough to grease surface. Cover with damp cloth and let rise in warmish spot till double.

Punch down and let rise again until dough holds impression of a finger, then punch down and divide into 3 parts. Form dough into loaves, place in pans, and brush with soft butter. Let rise double as oven preheats to 400 degrees. Bake 35-40 minutes or until bread is golden brown and sounds hollow when rapped on bottom with knuckles. Cool bread on racks. Wrap in foil. Makes 3 loaves.

To Pack: Bread and butter.

In Camp: Heat foil-wrapped loaf in steamer.

Strawberry Fool

1 pint strawberries	1 pint heavy cream
1-2 tablespoons sugar	1/4 cup confectioner's sugar
1 tablespoon creme de cassis	1 teaspoon vanilla

At Home: Puree strawberries in blender or food processor; add sugar and creme de cassis to taste. Whip cream and add confectioner's sugar and vanilla. Fold puree into cream. Keep very cold and transport in plastic container. This keeps for about 24 hours. If you need to keep it longer, bring the strawberry puree frozen, and whip cream in camp using volunteers. Makes 6-8 servings.

To Pack: Strawberry Fool (or strawberry puree and heavy cream).

In Camp: Serve cold in insulated cups.

5

Living Well on the Big Biloxi: Canoe Camping for Beginners

The Big Biloxi, running shallow and clear past white beaches and deep woods near Gulfport, Mississippi, is an ideal river for first-time canoeing. Particularly in late May when magnolias spill their sharp perfume and the sun glints through overhanging branches, it's a reassuring place for the timid or the untried. Unless it rains, of course. And even then it's not such a bad place to be.

The rains came just as my partner and I were readying our first-timers for launch from the Big Biloxi Campground. First a sprinkle, then a shower, the rain swiftly worked its way up to a marathon drenching that continued unabated for the next five hours. Oddly enough, the beginners didn't seem to mind—maybe they thought the weather was par for canoeing. Whatever the

Photo by Hulin Robert.

A quiet campground welcomes the evening sun.

case, their spirits remained drip-dry even as the moisture slowly invaded the unsealed seams of their city raincoats.

Toward evening the rain finally drizzled to a stop and we found refuge on a freshly-laundered beach. Once wrung-out, we were struck with a remarkable feeling: *it felt so unbelievably good— almost religiously so—to be out of the pelting rain.* Just to have stood there, un-rained-upon, would have been enough, but we had more—a Biblical sunset drenching our beach with orange and saffron light, a sumptuous dinner fresh from the garden, and finally, long hours of down-wrapped sleep. (And to this day, Mom still thinks camping means roughing-it.)

For information on the Big Biloxi:

National Forests in Mississippi
100 W. Capitol St., Suite 1141
Jackson, MS 39269
601/961-4391

Mississippi Department of
 Wildlife Conservation
P. O. Box 451
Jackson, MS 39205
601/961-5300

MENUS

(*indicates recipes given)

Breakfast

Stuffed Pancakes with Orange Sauce*
Grilled Smoked Sausage
Orange Quarters
Banana Chunks • Honeydew Slices • Cherries
Coffee • Milk

Lunch

Central Grocery Muffalettos*
Chocolate Chip Cookie Monsters*
Coffee

Dinner

Curried Stuffed Eggs* • Blanched Broccoli Flowerets
Big Biloxi Boiled Dinner* • Sesame Mayonnaise*
Pineapple Upside-Down Cake with Vanilla Whipped Cream*
Wine: A flowery white such as
Round Hill Fumé Blanc

Spring / Living Well on the Big Biloxi

Stuffed Pancakes With Orange Sauce

This recipe is worth the trouble it takes and never fails to win raves. An equally delicious, sexier sauce can be made of brandied cherries thickened slightly with cornstarch.

PANCAKES

2 cups all-purpose flour
1 teaspoon salt
3 teaspoons baking powder
2 cups milk

4 egg yolks, beaten
4 tablespoons melted butter
4 egg whites, stiffly beaten

FILLING

2 (8-ounce) packages cream cheese, softened

1/4 cup honey or brown sugar

SAUCE

1/2 stick butter
1/4 cup sugar or to taste
3 teaspoons cornstarch

Grated rind of 1 orange
  (about 1 heaping tablespoon)
2 cups fresh orange juice

At Home: For pancakes, mix dry ingredients; stir in milk, egg yolks, and melted butter. Fold in stiffly beaten egg whites. Bake pancakes on hot but not smoking griddle until golden brown. Set aside.

For filling, whip together cream cheese and honey or brown sugar. Spread each pancake with the mixture and roll it up. Stack rolled pancakes in a single layer in groups of 3 for each serving. Wrap serving in heavy foil and freeze, if desired.

For sauce, melt butter, add sugar, cornstarch, rind, and orange juice and whisk over low heat until mixture thickens slightly. Carry to camp in jar, refrigerated.

To Pack: Pancakes, sauce, tongs, steamer.

In Camp: Heat foil-wrapped pancakes in top of steamer. If you heat many at a time, it takes a while. Heat orange sauce separately. Serve pancakes in foil packs (tongs come in handy), and top with sauce. Serves 6 scrumptiously.

Central Grocery Muffalettos

These knock-out sandwiches can be made at home and carried along on a day trip. They are specialties of the Central Grocery across from the New Orleans French Market.

Provolone
Genoa salami

Baked ham
Italian bread (recipe below)

OLIVE SALAD

1/2 cup Greek black olives
1/2 cup Spanish pimento-
   stuffed olives
1/2 cup finely chopped celery

1 teaspoon oregano
1 tablespoon minced garlic
2 tablespoons chopped parsley
1 cup olive oil

At Home: Make olive salad by mixing olives, celery, oregano, garlic, parsley, and olive oil. Carry to camp in a widemouth jar.

To Pack: Olive salad, Italian Bread, Provolone, baked ham, Genoa salami.

In Camp: Split round loaves of Italian bread horizontally. Spread generously with olive salad and its oil. Layer thin slices of Provolone, baked ham, and Genoa salami. One sandwich serves one ravenous or two hungry people.

Italian Bread

This bread is crusty, flavorful, and quite simple to make, although store-bought Italian bread is lighter in texture.

2 cups warm water
1 package dry yeast
2 1/2 teaspoons salt
2 eggs, lightly beaten

3 tablespoons melted
   shortening
About 7 cups all-purpose
   flour

At Home: Pour water in large bowl, stir in yeast till dissolved. Add salt, eggs, and shortening, then add flour one cup at a time, stirring until you have a manageable dough.

Knead dough on floured board, adding more flour if dough is sticky, for 10-15 minutes. Dough should be light and pliable. Grease dough and put it in greased bowl covered with a damp cloth. Let rise until double. Punch down and form in two round loaves; place them on greased pan, and sprinkle with cornmeal.

Preheat oven to 375 degrees while dough rises almost double. Bake in oven with pan of hot water on lower shelf until bread is golden brown, about a half hour. Makes 2 round loaves.

Spring / Living Well on the Big Biloxi

Chocolate Chip Cookie Monsters

Use the recipe on the chocolate chip package, but use an ice cream scoop to measure dough and pat it into 5-inch rounds. Transport in Ziploc bags, or large cookie tin. These, along with hot coffee made at breakfast and stored in the thermos, will compensate for up to six hours of rain.

Curried Stuffed Eggs

12 small or medium-sized hard-boiled eggs	1 tablespoon scallions, minced
	1 tablespoon parsley, minced
1/3 cup mayonnaise (or enough to moisten)	1 tablespoon Dijon mustard
	Cayenne pepper to taste
1 teaspoon curry powder	

At Home: Peel eggs, cut in half crosswise, scoop out yolks, and cut a thin slice from bottom of eggs so they sit flat on plate. Mash yolks with remaining ingredients and blend well. You may add chopped white part of egg from the slices removed. Stuff back into whites and transport in styrofoam egg container or shallow plastic container.

To Pack: Curried Eggs, broccoli flowerets.

In Camp: Serve on platter with blanched broccoli flowerets. In the unlikely event you have leftover eggs, they make delicious sandwiches on buttered or mayonnaised bread with lettuce or sprouts. Makes 24 halves.

Big Biloxi Boiled Dinner

The success of this wonderful spring dish depends entirely on the pristine freshness of the vegetables. (Grow your own.)

2 pounds fresh firm, poachable
    fish such as salmon or redfish
Juice of 2 lemons
24 medium new potatoes
2 1/2 pounds fresh young
    green beans

16 fresh young carrots
2 sticks butter
1/2 cup minced parsley
1/2 cup minced chives or
    green onion tops
Salt and pepper to taste

At Home: Rinse fish and place in Ziploc freezer bag with lemon juice. Scrub vegetables and transport in Ziploc bags. Keep very cold.

To Pack: Fish, potatoes, carrots, beans, butter, parsley, chives, salt and pepper, steamer, covered skillet.

In Camp: Poach fish in lemon juice and water just to cover in covered skillet for 15 minutes, or till just done. Bring water to boil in bottom of steamer, add potatoes cut in fourths and carrots cut in chunks, cover. After 7 minutes, add beans in steamer section on top of potatoes and carrots and cover. Cook five minutes more or until all vegetables are just tender.

Meanwhile, drain fish, remove to foil and keep warm. Wipe out skillet with paper towel. Melt butter, add parsley and chives and pour over drained potatoes, carrots, and fish as each plate is served. Top each serving of beans with a dollop of Sesame Mayonnaise. Salt and pepper the whole dinner to taste.

You can substitute fresh shrimp for the fish or increase the quantity of vegetables and omit the fish altogether. Serves 6-8.

Sesame Mayonnaise

Try this on raw vegetables, salad, pasta, or sandwiches. It's truly addictive.

2 eggs
2 1/2 tablespoons rice or
    sherry vinegar
1 tablespoon Dijon mustard

1/4 cup sesame oil
2 1/2 cups vegetable oil
Oriental chili oil

At Home: In blender process eggs, vinegar, and mustard until blended. Dribble oil into egg mixture in a steady stream until oil is absorbed and mayonnaise is fluffy and thick. Remove from blender and season with chili oil to taste. Some like it hot. Makes 1 1/2 pints.

To Pack: Mayonnaise, wooden bowl.

In Camp: Serve on steamed green beans.

Pineapple Upside-Down Cake with Vanilla Whipped Cream

1 (20-ounce) can pineapple slices (pears, apples, and apricots also make excellent upside-down cake)
1/3 cup butter, melted
1/2 cup brown sugar
12 pecan halves
1 1/2 cups sifted all-purpose flour

1 cup sugar
2 teaspoons baking powder
3/4 teaspoon salt
1/3 cup butter
1/3 cup pineapple syrup
1/3 cup milk
1 teaspoon vanilla
1/4 teaspoon almond extract
1 egg

At Home: Drain pineapple, reserving syrup. Melt butter in bottom of 10-inch iron skillet. Stir in brown sugar. Arrange pineapple slices and pecans in skillet. Sift flour with sugar, baking powder, and salt. Add butter, pineapple syrup, milk, and flavorings. Beat 2 minutes at medium speed on mixer. Add egg and beat 2 minutes more. Pour batter over pineapple. Bake at 350 degrees about 50 minutes or until cake tests done. Let stand about 5 minutes before turning upside-down on waxed paper in cake tin.

To Pack: Cake, cream, vanilla.

In Camp: Warm cake by campfire and serve with vanilla-flavored whipped cream. If your cream-whippers get out of hand as ours did one dark night, the resulting butter they produce is delicious for breakfast. Serves 6-8.

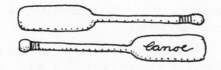

Spring / Living Well on the Big Biloxi

6

Little Cahaba Canoe and Gourmet Society: An Alabama Whitewater Excursion

In its exuberant trek through the hills of central Alabama, the Little Cahaba River skims through caves of leafy shade, pours in clear cascades over stone ledges, and in May blooms with acres of white swamp lilies: in all, a perfect setting for a meeting of the River Rats Canoe and Gourmet Society.

As the name implies, the Society dines as adventurously as it canoes, and on this trip simplified matters by assigning each member-couple a meal to plan, prepare, and serve. It was understood meals would meet the usual high standards of epicurean fast food.

Breakfast may seem elaborate, but took only 20 minutes from ice chest to picnic table, speeding us on our way from camp at Oak Mountain State Park (camping on the river is prohibited) to our shuttle at Bulldog Bend. Lunch, simple and plentiful, traveled in a small ice chest, and was arrayed on the plastic ground cloth inside of five minutes. And dinner was the usual prolonged and boistrous affair that typically follows a well-spent day on a challenging new river: part decompression, part celebration...all delicious.

For information on the Little Cahaba:

The Bulldog Bend Canoe Co.
205/926-7382

Shuttles, canoe rentals, river information.

Alabama Bureau of Tourism
and Travel
523 S. Perry Street
Montgomery, AL 36104

Camping at Oak Mountain State Park

<h1 style="text-align:center">MENUS</h1>

(*indicates recipes given)

Breakfast

Country Style Ham and Cream Gravy*
Soft Rolls and Raspberry Jam
Sour Cream Coffee Cake*
Citrus Compote*
Coffee

Lunch

Brie and Kavli*
Kippers, Sliced Vidalia Onion, and Lemon Wedges*
Miss Kit's Poppyseed Cake* • Oranges • Cherries
Perrier

Dinner

Cucumber Dill Salad*
Polish Cabbage Rolls*
Gran's Pot Roast*
Dark Rye Bread
Sinfully Chocolate Cake*
Heineken Beer

Country Style Ham and Cream Gravy

2 tablespoons butter	3 tablespoons flour
2 pounds 1/4-inch thick	2 cups light cream
smoked ham steaks	Salt, pepper and sage to taste

At Home: Melt butter in skillet, add ham, and fry slowly for 5 minutes. Remove ham, add flour and blend; add cream and whisk to blend. Cook 5 minutes, then add ham and season to taste using lots of pepper, a little salt, a hint of sage. Simmer gently till gravy thickens. Carry to camp in plastic container or Ziploc freezer bag.

To Pack: Ham, milk or cream.

In Camp: Heat ham in gravy, adding milk or cream if necessary. This dish is a natural with grits, particularly in cold weather. Serves 6-8.

Spring / Little Cahaba Canoe

61

Sour Cream Coffeecake

Only whitewater paddlers need hefty servings; small will do for everyone else. It's *rich*.

1 cup butter	1 teaspoon baking powder
2 cups sugar	1/4 teaspoon salt
2 eggs	1 cup chopped pecans
1 cup sour cream	4 teaspoons sugar
1/2 teaspoon vanilla	1 teaspoon cinnamon
2 cups all-purpose flour	

At Home: Cream butter and sugar until fluffy. Beat in eggs one at a time. Fold in sour cream and vanilla. Combine flour, baking powder, and salt; fold into batter. Spread 1/3 of batter in 10-inch bundt cake pan.

Combine pecans, remaining sugar and cinnamon and sprinkle 3/4 of mixture over batter in pan. Spoon in remaining batter; top with remaining pecan mixture. Bake at 350 degrees for 50 or 60 minutes, until cake tests done. Wrap entire cake and pan in foil.

To Pack: Cake.

In Camp: Serve warm by steaming foil-wrapped cake over boiling water. This cake is much better warm. Serves 10-14.

Citrus Compote

1 grapefruit	4 large sweet oranges

At Home: With a sharp knife, separate grapefruit and oranges into sections, removing most of the white membrane. Transport in wide-mouth jar.

To Pack: Citrus Compote.

In Camp: Serve ice cold in cups. Serves 6.

Brie and Kavli

An extravagant, elegant wedge of Brie is a treat and especially civilized in the wild, where not much else is. Serve it and the kippers on dark crisp Kavli.

Kippers, Sliced Vidalia Onion, and Lemon Wedges

Easy-to-carry canned kippers, smoked fish savored by Englishmen and us, are even better garnished with sliced Vidalia onions and tart lemon wedges.

Miss Kit's Poppyseed Cake

Unlike Miss Kit, this cake is old-fashioned, and not too sweet.

2 1/4 cups all-purpose flour	3 eggs, lightly beaten
1 1/2 cups sugar	1 1/4 cups milk
3/4 cup poppyseed	3/4 cup oil
1 tablespoon baking powder	1 tablespoon vanilla

At Home: Preheat oven to 350 degrees. Grease and sugar 2 loaf pans. Combine dry ingredients. Add combined beaten eggs, milk, and oil and mix well. Add vanilla and mix well. Bake 50-60 minutes until cake tests done. Wrap tightly in foil when cool. Makes 2 loaves.

To Pack: Cakes.

In Camp: Serve in thin slices.

Cucumber-Dill Salad

2 firm cucumbers, peeled unless homegrown, and sliced thin	2 green onions, minced
10 radishes, sliced thin	2 sprigs parsley, minced
1 cup sour cream	1 tablespoon sugar
2 tablespoons wine vinegar	1 tablespoon chopped fresh dill or 1 teaspoon dried

At Home: Mix ingredients and refrigerate in jar(s). This keeps for several days.

To Pack: Jar of salad.

At Camp: Serve as a first course in cups or as an accompaniment to the meal. Serves 4-6.

Polish Cabbage Rolls

Another dish easier than it sounds, and really easy to eat.

1 pound ground chuck or round	1 1/2 teaspoons paprika
1 medium onion, chopped	Water, if needed
3 green onions, chopped	2 eggs, beaten
2 stalks celery, chopped	8-10 large green outer
1 small green pepper, chopped	leaves of cabbage
2 large cloves garlic, chopped	2 cups canned whole or
2 cups cooked brown or white	fresh tomatoes, chopped
rice	1 bay leaf, crumbled
1 teaspoon salt or to taste	Juice of 1 lemon
1 teaspoon pepper or to taste	

At Home: Brown meat, then drain to remove all but 1 tablespoon fat. Set meat aside and cook vegetables in reserved fat until they are barely tender. Return meat to pan, then add cooked rice, salt, pepper, paprika, and a bit of water if it seems dry. Bind mixture with beaten eggs and cook about 3 minutes. Taste for seasoning.

Scald cabbage leaves in boiling water for 5 minutes. Fill leaves with meat mixture and roll up, tucking ends under. Place rolls in casserole and add tomatoes, crumbled bay leaf, and lemon juice. Bake, covered for 30 minutes at 300 degrees. Cool. Package individual servings of two or three rolls in heavy foil or Seal-a-Meal bags.

To Pack: Cabbage rolls, lemons, tongs, steamer.

In Camp: Steam foil packets over steamer or heat Seal-a-Meal bags in boiling water until very hot. In the case of the foil packets, this takes a while. Garnish each serving with lemon wedges—they heighten flavor dramatically. Makes about 8-10 rolls or 4-5 servings.

Gran's Chuck Roast

This was Sunday dinner in Hammond, America, from 1946 on.

6 pounds boneless chuck roast	1 stalk celery, chopped fine
Flour	1 carrot, chopped
Salt, pepper, cayenne to taste	3 large cloves garlic, minced
1 slice bacon	1/2 teaspoon thyme
1 green pepper, chopped fine	1 bay leaf
1 large onion, chopped fine	Water or stock

At Home: Rub meat with flour, salt, pepper, and cayenne. Fry bacon; set aside. *Slowly* brown meat in bacon fat until it is a rich brown. Add chopped vegetables and cook till soft, stirring. Add garlic, thyme, bay leaf, crumbled bacon, and water or stock to cover meat. Cover pot and simmer meat until it is falling-down tender (add more water or stock, if necessary). Carry to camp in Ziploc freezer bag, frozen if you like.

To Pack: Meat, horseradish, catsup.

In Camp: Reheat meat and gravy in large pot. Serve accompanied by prepared horseradish and catsup. I know...strange. But you have to eat it that way. Serves 6-8.

Sinfully Chocolate Cake

This is scrumptious, especially if you avoid overbaking.

14 ounces semi-sweet chocolate
3 tablespoons water
12 eggs, separated
2 cups sugar

3/4 pound plus 4 tablespoons
  butter, softened
1 cup all-purpose flour, sifted
Orange slices

At Home: Preheat oven to 325 degrees. Butter and sugar a 10-inch tubular pan. Break chocolate in pieces, place in double boiler with water and melt, whisking till smooth. Cool slightly. Beat egg yolks and sugar until thick, then fold in chocolate, stir in very soft butter, and fold in sifted flour. Mix gently. Beat egg whites until stiff, stir a large spoonful of chocolate mixture into whites, and mix well. Pour into chocolate mixture; fold whites quickly but thoroughly into mixture. Bake cake for 1 hour and 10 minutes or until tester comes out clean. Please don't scorch! Cool for 1/2 hour and carefully remove cake to foil-lined cake tin. Refrigerate. In cool weather, transport cake in cake tin; in warm weather, wrap cake quarters in heavy foil or Ziploc freezer bags and store in ice chest.

Serve garnished with orange slices.

To Pack: Cake, oranges.

In Camp: Go thou and sin a little. Serves 15.

7

Spring Weed-Eatin':
A Wild Foods Camp Outing

Euell Gibbons is gone now, but the spirit of the man who wrote *Stalking the Wild Asparagus* (see page 215) and other delightful wild food books goes with us on our annual spring weed-eatin' trip. The damp spring woods bordering Pushepatapa Creek in Washington Parish, Louisiana, provided good pickings on a mild Saturday in May, but almost any woods or field will do. And even though wild food takes a long time to pick, wash, and cook, dinner—when it finally appears—is all the better for being fresh...and free.

Carefully identifying the weeds that can safely become tasty tidbits.

MENUS

(*indicates recipes given)

Breakfast

Apple-Green Juice*
Sunday Best Boiled Eggs*
Bran Muffins • Wild Honey • Muscadine Preserves
Yaupon Tea*

Lunch

Wild Greens and Salami Sandwiches*
Hickory Nut Tea Cake*
Sarsaparilla or Root Beer

Dinner

Herbed Cheese on Nutted Wheat Crackers*
Gumbo Z'Herbes* • Boiled Rice
Strawberry and Grapefruit Salad*
Wild Jam Tart*
Wine: A spicy white like St. Francis Gewurztraminer

Apple-Green Juice

You'll have to cheat on this and make it at home, but it's tasty and bursting with health.

1 quart boiling water
1 quart mixed wild greens
(plaintain, violet, dock,
smilax, chickweed, etc.),
washed and drained
2 whole seedless oranges,
blended to pulp in blender

1/2 lemon, seeded and blended
to pulp, peel and etc.
1/4 cup honey or to taste
Apple juice, bottled or
frozen

At Home: Pour boiling water over greens, and simmer, covered, for 20 minutes. Strain, reserving greens and juice. Add orange and lemon pulp to hot juice and sweeten with honey. Puree greens 2 cups at a time in blender. Combine pureed greens and liquid and chill. Strain and add apple juice to make 1/2 gallon. Makes 1/2 gallon.

To Pack: Juice.

In Camp: Serve ice cold.

Sunday Best Boiled Eggs

During the Depression, as my dad tells it, his family of eight breakfasted on one boiled egg: Grandpa ate the egg and one lucky kid got the top.

To Pack: Eggs, cottage cheese, onion, celery salt, salt and pepper.

In Camp: Set eggs in cold water. Bring gently to boil, reduce heat and simmer about 5 minutes for just-boiled eggs. Serve plain with salt and pepper; or mashed with a spoon of cottage cheese, a topping of chopped onion, and a sprinkle of celery salt.

Yaupon Tea

If you can get around the name, yaupon (Ilex vomitoria) makes the best wild plant tea in North America. So said Euell Gibbons, and I, connoisseur of all tea, agree. Found throughout the South, the small dark green leaves are gathered, washed, and roasted in a very slow oven until dark and crumbly. Brew the tea just as you do with Oriental tea leaves. It tastes nearly as good.

Wild Greens and Salami Sandwiches

Just before setting this recipe down in final form (in early December), I tested it again, gathering greens on a walk through my yard. Oxalis, wild chives, violet, and chickweed made up the tasty bundle, so I recommend this recipe even in winter.

Wild greens; violet leaves, smilax tips, peppergrass, chickweed, henbit, dandelion, or oxalis (wood sorrel)
Wild garlic (can substitute green onion tops)

Crunchy bran bread
Cream cheese, softened
Tomato slices
Thin-sliced top quality salami

To Pack: Greens, garlic, or green onion, bread, cream cheese, tomato, salami.

In Camp: Wash and dry wild greens. Spread bread with softened cream cheese. Layer with wild greens, tender shoots of wild garlic or green onion, thin sliced tomatoes, and salami. This is also good on po-boy bread.

Hickory Nut Tea Cake

This tasty cake keeps well for at least a week, wrapped and refrigerated.

2 cups sugar
1 cup (2 sticks) butter,
  softened
2 cups all-purpose flour,
  sifted
1 cup ground hickory nuts

1/4 teaspoon salt
1 teaspoon vanilla
1 teaspoon lemon extract
  (this is important)
5 eggs, room temperature

At Home: Preheat oven to 350 degrees. Place ingredients in order in large bowl and beat at high speed for 5 minutes. Bake in greased, sugared 9 or 10-inch tube pan about an hour or until cake tests done. Cool 10 minutes and remove from pan. Transport in foiled-lined cake tin.

To Pack: Cake.

In Camp: Serve in thin slices. Makes 1 loaf.

Herbed Cheese on Nutted Wheat Crackers

This spread is also wonderful on warm bagels for brunch.

2 tablespoons fresh herbs,
  minced (parsley, chervil,
  dill, chives, etc.)
1/2 pound Feta cheese

1/2 pound cream cheese
1 tablespoon heavy cream
Cayenne
1 large clove garlic, minced

At Home: Process or whip in mixer all ingredients until blended. Keeps in refrigerator for a week. Makes 2 cups.

To Pack: Cheese, crackers, spreader.

In Camp: Serve on nutted wheat crackers; Pepperidge Farm makes good ones.

Spring / Spring Weed-Eatin'

Gumbo Z'Herbes

This is an old Creole recipe, adaptable to all kinds of garden or wild greens and much more delicious than it may sound.

2 quarts water
8 quarts wild or garden greens
   wild lettuce, chickweed,
   smilax, violets wild mustard,
   dock, peppergrass, poke, or
   mustard greens, turnip greens,
   radish greens, beet greens,
   parsley, carrot tops, broccoli leaves, lettuce, cabbage
   (as you can see, anything
   goes—the mixture's the thing)
2 tablespoons shortening

2 1/2 pounds pickled pork
   (ham can be substituted,
   or sausage, beef, chicken—
   even shrimp)
1 large onion, chopped
3 large cloves garlic, minced
1/2 teaspoon ground cloves
1 teaspoon thyme or to taste
2 bay leaves
Salt, cayenne, and pepper
   to taste

At Home or In Camp: Cook washed, cut-up greens in boiling water for 1 hour. Cut pork in 1-inch pieces, and saute in shortening until lightly browned. Add onion and garlic and saute until onion is clear. Drain greens, reserving liquor, and add to pork, onion, and garlic; saute mixture until greens are dry and faintly browned. Add seasoning to taste (make it hot!), add greens liquor, and simmer for 1 hour. Cool and transport in plastic container. The extra gumbo freezes just fine. Makes 2 quarts.

To Pack: All separately to cook in camp, or gumbo and rice if cooked at home.

In Camp: Heat and serve in plastic bowls with a big spoonful of Boiled Rice. Spring tonic par excellence!

Strawberry and Grapefruit Salad

At Home and To Pack:

Whole strawberries
Grapefruit

Mayonnaise
Boston or other soft lettuce

In Camp: Section grapefruit and toss with strawberries in mayonnaise thinned with a bit of extra strawberry and grapefruit juice. Serve on Boston or other soft lettuce.

Wild Jam Tart

Rich and buttery with a hidden surprise of tart jam inside.

2 sticks butter (no substitute)
1 cup sugar
1 1/2 teaspoons lemon rind
  (blackberry, raspberry, huck-
  elberry--make your own
  with 2 cups frozen or fresh
  berries, 1/2 cup sugar and
  1 cup water simmered till
  thick)

2 eggs
1 1/4 cups all-purpose flour
1/2 teaspoon cinnamon
1/4 teaspoon cloves
1/4 teaspoon salt
1 1/4 cups blanched almonds,
  ground to powder in blender
1 cup wild berry preserves
Confectioner's sugar

At Home: Preheat oven to 325 degrees. Cream butter and sugar until light. Add lemon rind and eggs and beat well. Sift flour, spices, and salt together; add along with almonds to butter mixture and blend well. With floured hands or a spoon, spread half of mixture into bottom of a 9-inch tart or cake pan. Spread preserves on top.

Spread remaining dough on top of preserves and bake for about 50 minutes or until top is evenly browned. Sprinkle top with confectioner's sugar. Cool and wrap tightly in foil.

To Pack: Tart.

In Camp: Heat over steam. Serves 6-8.

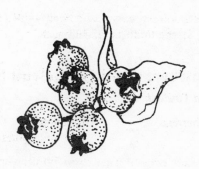

8

Splashing Down the Nantahala:
Whitewater Canoeing, Appalachian Style

Mountain grandmas, Olympic whitewater contenders, and plain old River Rats have a special place in their hearts for western North Carolina's Nantahala River. Dropping like a stone from the icy depths of Nantahala Lake, the Nanty plunges and foams eight miles through a noon-lit gorge, gathering strength and meanness for the coup de grace at Nantahala Falls.

Courtesy of the Nantahala Outdoor Center, Bryson City, NC.

Cold feet, high hearts—to paddle the Nantahala is to be alive!

On crowded spring weekends, Olympians and River Rats make room for each other. Playing the olympians with the river like a big rough pet, tossing it one elegant stroke to our ten, study each rapid in a classic quest for perfect technique. We River Rats, in contrast, merely strive to stay upright. Barreling through standing waves, doused with lapfuls of icy water, screaming into eddies, we grow happier and hungrier with each splashing, dashing mile, praying for strength and water enough for a second run.

The grandmas wait for us all at the Falls where they've set up lawn chairs to be entertained by the spectacle of the Rats, at least, frantically dodging cross currents, side-slipping around the snarling upper sousehole, and triumphantly low bracing into the terminal drop...or, alternatively, wiping out in some fresh and interesting way.

By the time we crawl out of the river for the second time, we've metabolized everything but our wool socks and could use a few thousand calories. If we're too tired to walk, let alone cook, help waits a few steps from the take-out where Aurelia Kennedy, co-founder and culinary genius of the Nantahala Outdoor Center, sets us right at Relia's Garden Restaurant with her featherweight biscuits, mountain-reared trout, and blueberry pies. Otherwise, we snake back up the mountain to Apple Tree Group Camp and light up the barbecue.

For information on canoeing Appalachian whitewater:

Nantahala Outdoor Center
U. S. 19W, Box 41
Bryson City, NC 28713
704/488-2175

Canoeing, kayaking, and rafting rentals and instruction; lodging, feasting.

District Ranger U.S. Forest
    Service
Route 1, Box 16-A
Robbinsville, NC 28771
701/479-6431

Apple Tree Group Camp and other campgrounds in the Natahala National Forest.

National Forests in North Carolina
P. O. Box 2750
Asheville, NC 28802
704/257-4200

Information on North Carolina campgrounds.

MENUS

(*indicates recipes given)

Breakfast

Tangerine Juice*
Borschburgers*
Coffee

Lunch

Tuna Pepper Buns*
Winesap Apples
Italian Fig Cookies
Ice Water

Dinner

Hummus* and Pita Bread
Lamb Shish Kebab*
Caroline's Fruit Salad* • Buttermilk Cake*
Mint Tea*
Wine: A light red with pizzazz such as
Fetzer Gamay Beaujolais

Tangerine Juice

Carry frozen concentrate and make it up in camp to save space.
It's a pleasant change from orange juice.

Borschburgers

You won't find a sloppier, more satisfying breakfast dish than this. It's protein-packed for long-lasting paddling energy.

For each serving:

1/4 pound ground chuck or turkey	1 egg
Salt and pepper	1 slice sharp Cheddar
Butter	Sliced onion
	Buttered sesame roll

At Home: Salt and pepper meat and form into plump patties. Wrap and freeze patties separately in plastic bag.

To Pack: Patties, rolls, butter, cheese, onion, eggs, two skillets.

In Camp: Butter buns, wrap in foil and set by fire or over steam to warm. Pan-fry patties on griddle or skillet until done to taste. Toward the end of cooking, top each patty with Cheddar cheese and cover pan to melt cheese. In another skillet fry eggs until whites are set. Put each cheese-topped burger on a warm buttered sesame roll, cover with onions, and top with a fried egg.

Tuna Pepper Buns

These will last through the morning unrefrigerated, stowed in a Ziploc freezer bag in a waterproof lunch bag or small ice chest in the canoe.

2 tablespoons olive oil	1 (9 1/4-ounce) can solid white albacore tuna, drained and flaked (no substitute)
1 tablespoon lemon juice	
1 recipe Peppers Provencal (add 1/2 cup broken Italian black olives)	4 fresh hard rolls (or 1 round Italian Bread)

At Home: Blend olive oil and lemon juice with Peppers Provencal.

To Pack: Rolls, Peppers Provencal, tuna.

In Camp: Spread one half of roll with a layer of Peppers Provencal and the other half with some of the liquid. Layer tuna on top of peppers and wrap sandwich in foil. Makes 4 sandwiches.

Hummus

This is a comforting dip, but a little too easy to eat. You wouldn't want to find yourself alone with a pint of it on a lonely Saturday night. Or would you?

2 cups canned garbanzo beans,
   drained
1/4 cup tahini (sesame paste)
3 tablespoons water
2 tablespoons olive oil

Juice of large lemon
2 or more garlic cloves,minced
3/4 teaspoon salt
Pepper to taste

At Home: Combine garbanzo beans, tahini, water, olive oil, and lemon juice in food processor or blender until smooth. If you use blender, blend small amounts. Add garlic, salt, and pepper to your taste. This freezes well.

   Note: I hope you taste your food as you cook, and trust yourself at least as much as you trust the fallible recipe in front of you! Makes 1 dangerous pint.

To Pack: Hummus, pita bread.

In Camp: Dip up the Hummus with pita bread.

Lamb Shish Kebab

Leg of lamb (about 3 1/2
   pounds meat, boned and
   cut in 1 1/2 -inch cubes)
   Unless you went to
   meatcutter's school,
   let your butcher do this.
1 cup olive oil
1/3 cup wine vinegar
Juice of 2 lemons
1 mild white onion, thinly
   sliced

5 thin slices lemon
2 teaspoons oregano
1 teaspoon freshly-ground
   black pepper
2 pounds small new potatoes
1 pound small whole onions
2 large bell peppers
1 small eggplant
8 ounces fresh whole
   mushrooms
Salt

At Home: Mix marinade, using ingredients from olive oil through black pepper and pour over lamb in wide-mouth plastic jar or plastic container. Refrigerate for up to two days before trip, and give the jar an occasional headstand to distribute marinade.

To Pack: Lamb, potatoes, onions, bell peppers, eggplant, mushrooms, salt, skewers, charcoal, starter, grill.

Spring / Splashing Down the Nantahala

In Camp: Parboil potatoes till barely tender. Alternate with lamb, onions, bell pepper cubes, unpeeled eggplant chunks, and mushrooms on skewers. Using a handful of paper towels, brush skewer contents with marinade. Broil on grill over coals, basting often. Since the vinegar and lemon juice have all but cooked the lamb, not much more is necessary, just enough to brown meat and crisp-cook vegetables. After cooking, salt and serve. Serves 6-8.

Note: Assign the fire to an expert and leave loading and cooking of skewers to prospective consumers. Be generous in figuring quantities for this dish.

Caroline's Fruit Salad

2 naval oranges
2 large fresh sweet-smelling
   peaches or nectarines or
1 (10-ounce) package frozen
   peaches
1 pint strawberries

1 fresh ripe sweet-smelling
   pineapple
1 (10-ounce) box frozen
   blueberries
1 pint sour cream
Brown sugar

To Pack: Ingredients listed above.

In Camp: Peel and slice orange, slice peaches, hull strawberries, and cut peeled pineapple in chunks. Mix all fruits gently with the sour cream and sprinkle top with brown sugar. For that "hostess-with-the-mostest" touch, serve in the hollowed-out pineapple. Serves 6.

Spring / Splashing Down the Nantahala

Buttermilk Cake

Here's a cake that not only tastes great warm, but keeps on getting better. Serve it dressed up with fruit salad or plain for lunch or breakfast.

2 sticks butter (no substitute)   1/3 teaspoon soda
3 cups sugar   1/4 teaspoon salt
5 large eggs   3 cups sifted all-purpose flour
1 cup real buttermilk

At Home: Cream butter and sugar until they are creamy as mayonnaise. Separate eggs; beat yolks creamy and add to butter mixture. Add soda to 1/2 cup buttermilk and salt to other 1/2 cup. Add to butter mixture alternately with flour. Beat whites stiff but not dry. Fold into cake. Bake in tube pan buttered and sugared on bottom only at 350 degrees for an hour and 10 minutes or until cake tests done. Do not overbake! Leave in pan 10 minutes, then remove and wrap in foil. Transport in cake tin.

To Pack: Cake.

In Camp: Serve in generous slices topped with Caroline's Fruit Salad. Serves about 12.

Mint Tea

Tea leaves   Fresh mint leaves
Honey

At Home: Make a strong essence of tea using an inexpensive brand since the mint overpowers the quality of the tea leaves. Sweeten the essence with honey and add a generous quantity of fresh mint leaves. Lacking mint, add a few spoons of mint tea when making the essence.

To Pack: Mint tea.

In Camp: Add water and ice. If you don't have fresh mint, you may find a sprig growing at the Nantahala's edge.

9

Easter on Horn Island:
A Wilderness Island Holiday

Of all the gifts of Horn Island—the white sand, the black lagoons, the ospreys, the crashing waves, and the silence—the most valuable is the gift of time. From the moment you splash ashore on this loveliest of the Gulf Islands National Seashore, time is yours and the long, slow hours from sunrise to moonset are yours to fill.

We spent our best Easter on Horn Island living as we pleased and not as usual. Setting our biological clocks to the rhythm of sun and moon, routine notions like "bedtime" and "breakfast," "lunch," and "dinner" were laid aside. Instead of breakfast, we walked miles down the broad Gulf beach, returning at mid-morning for brunch under the pines. In the hot midday we stretched out on lounge chairs with novels we'd finally found time to read. Toward late afternoon, we gathered improperly in our bathing suits for a completely proper tea—sandwiches, pastry, and perversely refreshing cups of hot Earl Grey. Then a swim and a stroll in the neon pink of sunset, and no one minded that supper came late...we'd taken time to watch the moonrise over Mississippi Sound.

For information on camping at Horn Island:

Asst. Superintendent, Gulf   Camping, boat shuttle.
  Islands National Seashore
3500 Park Road
Ocean Springs, MS 39564

Sea Grant Advisory Service   Boat charter.
4646 Beach Blvd., Suite 1-E
Biloxi, MS 39531
601/388-4701

On the beaches of Horn Island, time matters not at all.

MENUS
(*indicates recipes given)

Beach Brunch

Kiwi Spritzers*
Camp Eggs Sardou*
Brioche* • Strawberry Butter*
Persian Melon and Cherries
Amaretto Flavored Coffee

An Almost Proper Tea

A Trio of Tea Sandwiches*
Apricot Cheese Pastries*
Fortnum & Mason Earl Grey Tea

Moonlight Supper

Group Grope Salad*
Surfside Seafood Gumbo* • Boiled Rice
Garlic Bread
Delicate Orange Cheesecake*
Coffee
Wine: An elegant peachy white such as Estancia Chardonnay

Kiwi Spritzers

White wine   Kiwi slices, peeled
Club soda

To Pack: Wine, club soda, kiwis, plastic wine glasses.

In Camp: Combine equal portions of ice cold white wine and club soda in an insulated cup or plastic wine glass. Float slices of kiwi on top.

Spring / Easter on Horn Island

Camp Eggs Sardou

2 (10-ounce) packages frozen
chopped spinach
1 (10-ounce) package frozen
artichoke hearts
2 (10 1/2-ounce) cans Emilio's
Hollandaise Sauce (or make
your own)

Salt, pepper, and cayenne
to taste
6 jumbo eggs
Holland rusks (optional)

At Home: Cook spinach in scant water until water returns to boiling. Drain thoroughly and press out excess water. Cook artichoke hearts according to directions and cut into fourths. Mix 1 can Hollandaise with vegetables and season with salt, pepper, and cayenne. Transport in Ziploc freezer bags.

To Pack: Spinach mixture, eggs, covered skillet, Holland rusks.

In Camp: In large skillet, warm spinach mixture. Make wells with spoon and drop in eggs. Cover pan and steam eggs till tops are set. Serve immediately on warmed Holland rusks, topped with extra heated sauce. Serves 6.

Brioche

These fancy French buns are easy to make but expensive to buy.

2 packages dry yeast
6 tablespoons very warm water
in a cup
1/2 teaspoon salt
1 tablespoon sugar

4 cups all-purpose flour
1 tablespoon sugar
1 1/2 teaspoons salt
6 large eggs
3 sticks butter, very soft

At Home: Combine yeast, warm water, 1/2 teaspoon salt and 1 tablespoon sugar in a cup. Blend flour, remaining sugar and salt, eggs, and yeast mixture until well-combined. Blend in softened butter until dough is smooth. Let rise in a clean bowl in refrigerator or other under 70-degree spot until almost double.

Stir dough, and spoon into buttered muffin tins. Let rise again till almost double and bake at 475 degrees until browned, about 12-15 minutes. Cool and freeze in Ziploc bags. Makes 16 muffin-size brioche.

To Pack: Brioche, Strawberry Butter, steamer.

In Camp: Gently reheat in steamer and serve with Strawberry Butter or butter.

Strawberry Butter

1/2 cup butter   1/2 teaspoon lemon juice
1/3 cup excellent strawberry jam

At Home: Blend ingredients. Freeze if you make it more than a few days ahead. Serve on warmed brioche.

A Trio of Tea Sandwiches

Bacon, Pepper, and Pecan Tea Sandwiches:

2 cups finely crumbled crisp   1 cup finely chopped pecans
  bacon   Mayonnaise
1/4 cup finely chopped   Thin-sliced whole wheat
  green pepper   sandwich bread

At Home: Mix bacon, bell pepper, and pecans together. Add mayonnaise until of spreadable consistency, using a food processor if you have one.

To Pack: Bacon mixture, mayonnaise, bread.

In Camp: Spread bread with mayonnaise and bacon mixture and cut into fourths. Arrange on a tray. Makes 10-12 whole sandwiches or 40-48 tea sandwiches.

Cucumber Tea Sandwiches:

1 (8-ounce) package cream   Salt
  cheese, softened   Cucumbers, unwaxed with
Milk   skin, if possible
2 tablespoons minced chives   Thin-sliced white sandwich
  or green onion   bread

At Home: Whip cream cheese with milk until of spreading consistency. Add chives or green onion and salt to taste.

To Pack: Cream cheese mixture, cucumbers, bread.

In Camp: Spread bread with cream cheese, cut into fourths, and top with thinly-sliced cucumbers. Makes about 40 tea sandwiches.

Brown Bread and Butter Tea Sandwiches:

To Pack: Canned Boston Brown Bread, unsalted butter.

In Camp: Slice bread thin, spread with butter, and cut in half.

Spring / Easter on Horn Island

Apricot Cheese Pastries

2 cups sifted all-purpose flour
  flour
1/4 teaspoon salt
1 cup butter

1 (8-ounce) package cream
  cheese
Apricot preserves
Sugar

At Home: Sift flour and salt, add butter and cream cheese in small pieces. Cut butter and cheese into flour with pastry blender or electric mixer. Shape dough in ball, wrap, and refrigerate. Grease 2 cookie sheets and preheat oven to 400 degrees. Take golfball-sized pieces of dough, flatten between palms into 1/8-inch rounds. Place small dab apricot preserves in center of round, fold in half, and seal edges with fork. Sprinkle pastries with sugar, bake 10-12 minutes until very lightly browned, and cool. Transport in plastic container and keep cool till served. Makes about 24.

To Pack: Pastries.

In Camp: Remove from ice chest 1/2 hour before serving.

Group Grope Salad

An ideal salad to eat by moonlight...mano a' mano.

1 head iceberg lettuce
1 bag spinach
1 bunch parsley
2 cups cherry tomatoes, halved
4 green onions
2 cups small radishes
1/2 small cauliflower in
  flowerets

1 small jar almond-stuffed
  olives
2 small jars marinated
  artichoke hearts
1 1/2 cups oil-packed
  black olives
12 Italian pickled peppers

DRESSING

1 cup olive oil
2 tablespoons wine vinegar
2 cloves garlic, put through
  press

1 teaspoon oregano
Salt and pepper

At Home: Make dressing. Wash vegetables and place in Ziploc bags.

To Pack: Salad ingredients and dressing.

In Camp: Break lettuce in chunks, tear spinach to bite size. Chop parsley and cut onion in 3-inch pieces. Cut radishes in half. Drain olives, artichoke hearts, and peppers. Place all in large bowl and pour dressing over, just enough to cover vegetables after tossing. Eat this by hand with family or real good friends. Serves 8-10.

Surfside Seafood Gumbo

1/2 cup oil
1/2 cup all-purpose flour
1 green pepper, chopped
1 bunch green onions, chopped
2 stalks celery, chopped
1 large onion, chopped
4 large cloves garlic, chopped
1 teaspoon thyme
2 bay leaves
1 pound okra, sliced thin
2 strips lean bacon, chopped
1/4 cup chopped ham
1/4 cup parsley, minced
2 cups tomato juice or tomatoes
  and juice

6 cups chicken or shrimp stock
  (made from boiling shrimp
  shells)
1 pound shrimp, shelled
1 pint oysters and liquor
1 pound crab meat or 6 small
  gumbo crabs, in pieces
1 teaspoon salt or to taste
1/2 teaspoon cayenne
1/2 teaspoon pepper
1 teaspoon garlic powder
3 tablespoons file powder

At Home: Make a roux of oil and flour, cooking it dark brown, stirring constantly. Add green pepper, green onions, celery, onion, and garlic to roux and cook 5 minutes. Add thyme, bay leaves, okra, bacon, and ham, and cook 10 minutes more. Add parsley, tomato juice or tomatoes, and stock and cook for 45 minutes on low heat. Add shrimp, oysters and liquor, crab, salt, cayenne, pepper, and garlic powder and cook for 10 minutes.

Cool, freeze, if you like and transport to camp in wide-mouth plastic jar or Ziploc freezer bags.

To Pack: Gumbo, Boiled Rice, and file powder.

In Camp: Heat gumbo almost to boiling and add file powder. Serve over Boiled Rice in plastic bowls or cups and prepare to refill them more than once. Serves 6-8.

Delicate Orange Cheesecake

You'll never eat a plain cheesecake by choice once you've tried this.

1 1/2 cup graham cracker
  crumbs
1/4 cup ground walnuts or
  pecans
2 tablespoons brown sugar
1 teaspoon cinnamon
1/2 stick butter, melted

2 cups sour cream
3 (8-ounce) packages cream
  cheese
3 eggs, beaten
1 cup sugar
2 teaspoons vanilla
Grated peel of 1 orange

At Home: Preheat oven to 375 degrees. Combine crumbs, nuts, brown sugar and cinnamon; add butter and mix. Reserve 2 tablespoons for top of cake and press remainder into bottom and sides of a 9-inch cake pan.

Combine sour cream, cream cheese, eggs and sugar in food processor, blender, or bowl of electric mixer, and whip till smooth. Add vanilla and orange peel and mix.

Bake for 50 minutes. Sprinkle reserved topping on cake and bake for another 10 minutes. Let cool, wrap in foil and a large freezer bag and keep cold.

To Pack: Cheesecake.

In Camp: Serve with coffee. Makes 8 servings.

Spring / Easter on Horn Island

Summer

A carefree float on the river cools a summer afternoon.

1

Coming of Age on the Amite:
The Great Kids' Canoe Trip

Smarting at banishment from the last canoe trip, an adults-only assault on Georgia/South Carolina's Chattooga River, the River Rats' kids, then ranging from 6 to 12 years old, were wild for a trip of their own. It would be the Great Kids' Canoe Trip, and adults would be banished—from kids' boats, at least. In exchange, the young fry magnanimously agreed to help plan the food.

Agreeable but cautious, we chose for the epic event a quiet stretch of the Amite River, as scenic as the neighboring Tangipahoa; but spared, thanks to the remoteness of its upper stretches, the Tangi's mad tangle of summer tubers and rental canoes. When we arrived at the Darlington, Louisiana bridge, the river

to by Mike Osborne.

After years of apprenticeship, at last, a boat of their own!

89

was running clear with a fine current, and a fresh breeze moderated the heat already pouring from a washed blue sky.

The day passed through a haze of sun and greenwater swimming, in sunscreen rubs on tender shoulders, in a six-year-old's fit spotting a watersnake swimming with a hapless fish in its mouth—"Somebody saaaave the poor fish!"—and in chasing green herons around a backwater pond. But the most interesting part came last.

Approaching a blind curve, the river suddenly narrowed and shot through a tangle of fallen trees, catching the lead boat unaware. It rammed a submerged stump, flipped sideways, filled up, and was gone, leaving its adult crew breast-stroking abashedly in its wake. And then came the kids. Nine-year-old Johnny first with his bow-lady Robin; both calmly ignored the shouted, conflicting instructions and negotiated the maze perfectly—backward, but perfectly. The rest of the kid's more or less followed suit, and after that, barbequed burgers and brownies later in camp were nothing but anticlimax.

MENUS
(*indicates recipes given)

Breakfast
Evadne's Gingerbread and Butter*
Miniature Smoked Sausages
Pineapple and Banana Kabobs*
Strawberry Milk* • Coffee for Adults

Lunch
Apple-Baked Ham Sandwiches*
Peanut Butter Cookies* • Watermelon Chunks
Dad's Orangeade*

Dinner
Mexican Vegetable Salad Bowl* • Cajun Johnnyburgers*
Bobbie's Fudge Brownies*
Natural Flavor Soft Drinks for Kids • Beer for Adults

Evadne's Gingerbread and Butter

This is the best gingerbread you'll ever taste, great for snacks or served warm with bourbon-flavored whipped cream—superb for dessert.

3 eggs	1 cup oil
1 cup sugar	2 teaspoons baking soda
1 cup molasses	2 tablespoons hot water
1 teaspoon each powdered	2 cups all-purpose flour
clove, ginger, and cinnamon	1 cup boiling water

At Home: In large bowl mix with mixer, eggs, sugar, molasses, spices, and oil. Dissolve 2 teaspoons baking soda in 2 tablespoons hot water and add to spice mixture. Stir in flour and beat well, add boiling water and beat lightly and quickly till mixed. Pour into greased 9x13-inch sugared pan and bake 35-45 minutes at 350 degrees or until gingerbread tests done in center.

To Pack: Gingerbread and butter.

In Camp: Serve cold with butter. Serves 6-8.

Pineapple and Banana Kabobs

Fresh pineapple chunks   Banana chunks

To Pack: Pineapple, bananas, toothpicks or skewers.

In Camp: Alternate fruit on toothpicks or small wooden skewers and serve at once. If they must wait, dip bananas in pineapple juice.

Strawberry Milk

Bring enough of this for adults, too.

2 tablespoons strawberry   1 cup cold milk
   puree

At Home: Make puree by whirring 1 (10-ounce) package frozen or 1 pint fresh sugared strawberries in blender.Combine 1 cup cold milk and 2 tablespoons strawberry puree per serving and transport in jar or plastic pitcher. Makes one serving.

To Pack: Strawberry milk.

In Camp: Serve ice cold. Makes one serving.

Apple-Baked Ham Sandwiches

This is such a wonderful ham recipe, I'll pass it on even though we're making sandwiches.

1 Cure 81 or other high-quality ham	Whole cloves
2 cups white wine	3/4 cup dark corn syrup
Water to cover ham	2/3 cup orange marmalade
4 cooking apples, cut in half	1 tablespoon brandy
2 sticks cinnamon	Yellow mustard
10 whole cloves	Mayonnaise
1 bay leaf	Thin-sliced rye
1 teaspoon dried basil or 1 sprig fresh	Tomato
	Lettuce

At Home: Place ham in large pot and add ingredients from wine through basil. Bring mixture to boil, then let simmer 1 hour. Let sit overnight (in marinade) in refrigerator. Next day, drain, saving marinade. Place ham on rack in baking pan. Attach halved apples from marinade with toothpicks. Bake at 300 degrees for 30 minutes, adding marinade if ham threatens to scorch. Remove from oven, remove apples, score skin into diamond shapes. Combine corn syrup, orange marmalade, and brandy and rub half mixture over ham. Insert whole cloves into center of each diamond. Bake 10 minutes at 450 degrees. Spread remaining glaze over ham and bake another 10 minutes, adding marinade if necessary.

To Pack: Ham, yellow mustard, mayonnaise, thin-sliced rye, tomato, lettuce, tray.

In Camp: Arrange thin-sliced ham (always slice sandwich meats paper thin,*) rye bread, mustard, mayonnaise, thin-sliced tomatoes, and lettuce on tray and watch it all disappear.

*Butchers will do it for you post-cooking if you're a regular.

Peanut Butter Cookies

Every standard cookbook has a delicious (probably the same) recipe for peanut butter cookies. I like to use chunky peanut butter in the recipe. For an adult trip, try Almond Butter Cookies, substituting almond butter for peanut butter. Almond butter costs more, but anything that good ought to.

Dad's Orangeade

On sultry summer nights before air conditioning, nothing cooled off his sweaty kids like Dad's Orangeade. Still does.

Fresh orange juice
Orange slices
Sugar to taste

Water
Ice

At Home: Squeeze orange juice and sugar it to taste. Transport in juice bottle.

To Pack: Orange juice, extra oranges for garnish, water.

In Camp: Fill cup half full of orange juice, add ice and water to fill cup and garnish with orange slice.

Mexican Vegetable Salad Bowl

Serve this piquant salad while the burgers are grilling.

1 (1-pound) can red beans, rinsed and drained
1 cup peeled and diced cucumber
1/2 cup diced green pepper
1 cup minced green onions
1 cup chopped celery
1/2 cup mayonnaise
1 tablespoon chopped jalapeno, (optional)

2 cloves garlic, minced
Juice of 1/2 lemon
4 teaspoons chili powder
Salt and pepper to taste
3 slices bacon, cooked crisp and crumbled
2 medium tomatoes, chopped and drained
1 small avocado, cubed (optional)

At Home: Mix all ingredients through salt and pepper. Transport salad in plastic covered salad bowl and bacon in Ziploc bag.

To Pack: Salad, bacon, tomatoes, and avocado.

In Camp: Mix tomato and avocado gently into salad and top with bacon. Makes 4-6 servings.

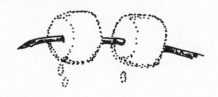

Summer / Coming of Age on the Amite

Cajun Johnnyburgers

My son Johnny, the burger specialist, offers this recipe, ideal for camping since it's preseasoned and the cheese melts internally and neatly if you do it right.

1/2 cup finely chopped onion
2 pounds ground chuck or
   turkey (if you use turkey,
   bring some oil for frying)
1 teaspoon salt
1/2 teaspoon pepper
1/4 teaspoon paprika
Pinch garlic powder
4 slices or 1 cup grated
   Cheddar cheese

4 Kaiser or other crisp
   bakery rolls
Mayonnaise
Creole mustard
Thick slices tomato
Thin slices mild onion
Lettuce
Garlic pickles

At Home: Mix onion, meat and seasoning in bowl. Form into 8 thin patties and put two together with a slice or 1/4 cup grated cheese between them. Freeze in Ziploc bag, separating patties with pieces of waxed paper.

To Pack: Seasoned burgers, 4 Kaiser or other crisp bakery rolls wrapped in foil, mayonnaise, Creole mustard, tomato, onion, lettuce, garlic pickles.

In Camp: Grill patties over coals or pan-fry them on griddle. Heat foil-wrapped buns on grill or in steamer. Arrange the sliced tomato, onion, and pickles with lettuce leaves on a platter, and let each burger fan take it from there. Makes 4 large burgers.

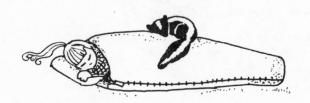

Bobbie's Fudge Brownies

My friend Bobbie O'Neil assures me these brownies contribute to health, so don't stint.

4 squares unsweetened chocolate	1 teaspoon vanilla
2 sticks butter	2 cups walnuts
2 cups sugar	1/2 cup wholewheat flour
4 large eggs	1 tablespoon nutritional yeast (optional)

At Home: Melt chocolate and butter in heavy saucepan large enough to mix brownies. Remove from heat and stir in sugar. Then beat in eggs and vanilla. Stir in walnuts, wholewheat flour and wheat germ. Spread batter in 9x11-inch buttered pan. Bake at 325 degrees for 40 minutes or until brownies are just shrinking from sides of pan. Do not overbake or they will be impossible to remove from pan. Cool and cut in squares and carry in cake tin.

To Pack: Brownies and milk, of course.

In Camp: Makes 10-12 generous servings.

2

Mandeville Fourth of July:
A Lakefront Houseparty

The 200th anniversary of our country's independence, July 4, 1976, was a rocketing success in Mandeville, Louisiana, thanks to our audacity in inviting a crowd of friends to bring tents, sleeping bags, bicycles, boats, and food and join us in celebration amid the unopened cartons of the lakefront cottage into which we had moved the day before.

The Fourth dawned stifling hot and hazy, Lake Pontchartrain was motionless and warm as milk, and still they all came—and did the day proud. One couple christened our creaky old porch with a starchy American flag; Captain J. P. Wiggin skied all comers behind his Ascension Parish Sheriff's boat (secondhand, but it bought us respect in conservative Mandeville); we all collaborated cooking and eating the extravagant, non-stop buffet; and just at noon, a parade rolled by the front door!

(You can join Mandeville's Fourth of July festivities if you camp at nearby Fairview or Fontainebleau State Parks.)

For information on camping at Fairview or Fontainebleau:

Department of Culture, Recreation and Tourism
Office of State Parks
P. O. Drawer 1111
Baton Rouge, LA 70821
504/925-3830

MENUS

Lazy Morning Breakfast

Egg-Stuffed French Rolls*
Sliced Tomatoes • Peppers Provencal • Crumbled Bacon
Green Onion Tops • Cheshire Cheese
Strawberry Kiwi Bowl*
Wake-Up Iced Tea*

All-Day Buffet

Non-Stop Vegetable Platter* with Curry Mayonnaise* and
Salsa Verde* • Sprimp Remoulade*
Barbequed Beef Filet* • Apricot-Glazed Ham*
Persian Eggplant*
Cheese Board* • Butter Rolls
Gail's Rum Cake*
Bobbie's Fudge Brownies • Peach Ice Cream
Wine: A selection of light, inexpensive white and red such as
B&G Partager Vin Blanc and Vin Rouge
Much Beer, Iced Tea and Club Soda
Sliced Lemon, Lime, and Orange for Impromptu Sangria

Egg-Stuffed French Rolls

Pistolettes, baguettes, or crusty hard rolls	Sliced tomatoes
Eggs and cream	Peppers Provencal
Butter	Cheshire cheese
Salt and pepper	Crumbled bacon
	Green onion tops

At Home or In Camp: As your guests drift into the kitchen, let each fix his or her own version of Egg-Stuffed French Rolls. Make sure several non-stick skillets are on hand along with; fresh eggs, heavy cream, and bowls of sliced homegrown tomatoes, Peppers Provencal, Cheshire cheese, crumbled bacon, and green onion tops.

To Pack: Rolls, eggs, cream, butter, salt, pepper, tomatoes, Peppers Provencal, bacon, green onion tops.

Strawberry Kiwi Bowl

Whole strawberries   Kiwis
Sugar

At Home or In Camp: Slice peeled kiwis into an attractive bowl; add whole strawberries and a sprinkle of sugar.

To Pack: Strawberries, kiwis, sugar.

Wake-Up Iced Tea

Instead of serving hot tea or coffee on a sweltering hot summer morning, serve an icy pitcher of tea sparked with sliced lemon and lime.

At Home: Make strong tea, add sliced lemon and lime, and transport in clean gallon milk jug in the ice chest.

To Pack: Tea.

In Camp: Serve tea over ice. This is a refreshing breakfast drink for warm-weather beach or river camping; and so is iced coffee.

Non-Stop Vegetable Platter

Fresh raw vegetables are wonderfully suited for large group summer camp meals. Try any or all of the following on your enameled lightweight trays.

Radishes (red or white)
Broccoli flowerets (best if blanched briefly)
Carrot strips or curls (put thin shavings in ice water)
Cherry tomatoes, (cut in half to cut down on ricocheting)
Celery sticks
Green onions, (cut in half lengthwise)
Whole white mushrooms (only those with fresh alabaster complexions)
Zucchini slices
Young turnip slices (sweet and surprisingly good)
Beet slices (ditto)
Yellow squash slices (colorful and unexpected)
Green, red and yellow pepper rings
Cauliflower flowerets
Young green beans
Jicama (that strange brown vegetable you've always wondered about)

Summer / Mandeville Fourth of July

At Home and To Pack: Store vegetables—washed, trimmed, and peeled—in Ziploc bags with a squirt of fresh lemon juice to keep flavors lively. Interesting additions are pickled okra, pickled mirlitons, pickled peppers, and good black, ripe green, and stuffed olives. Serve wooden bowls of Curry Mayonnaise and Salsa Verde.

Curry Mayonnaise

1 cup good-quality mayonnaise, Hellman's or homemade
1 teaspoon grated fresh ginger
1 clove garlic, crushed
1/2 teaspoon salt
2 tablespoons chopped green onion
2 teaspoons curry powder
Juice of 1/2 lemon

At Home: Mix ingredients and chill in a jar. Makes about 1 1/4 cups.

Salsa Verde

2 cups firmly packed parsley leaves
1 large garlic clove
1 hard-boiled egg
2 anchovy fillets, rinsed and dried
1 tablespoon drained capers
1 small onion, chopped
1/3 cup red wine vinegar
1 cup olive oil
Salt and pepper to taste

At Home: In blender or food processor, puree all ingredients but olive oil; then add oil in a stream until blended. Season to taste. Chill in a jar. Makes 1 2/3 cups.

In Camp: Arrange vegetables on trays early and keep them replenished. Serve dipping sauce in wooden bowls.

Summer / Mandeville Fourth of July

Shrimp Remoulade

Modestly I report, this is the best shrimp remoulade on earth.

1 pound shrimp, boiled till
  just firm (about 5 minutes)
  and peeled
2 cloves garlic, minced
1/3 cup Creole mustard
2 tablespoons catsup
1 tablespoon paprika
1/4 teaspoon cayenne

1 teaspoon salt
1/3 cup tarragon vinegar
1/2 cup oil
1/2 cup chopped green
  onion
1 cup chopped celery
Shredded lettuce

At Home: Mix sauce ingredients; add boiled shrimp (cut in pieces, if large), green onions, and celery. Chill in widemouth jar.

To Pack: Shrimp and lettuce.

In Camp: Serve shrimp on a plate of cold shredded lettuce as an appetizer. Minus the shrimp, the sauce is good on cold, barely cooked cauliflower. Serves 6.

Barbequed Beef Filet

The kindest cut of all, a filet of beef is a treat for special people on a special day. Allow about 1/4 pound per person since you're also serving ham.

At least a 5-pound filet
  or a whole one, if possible
Butter

Salt and pepper
Parsley

At Home or In Camp: Trim fat and sinew and cut off about 6-inches of the tail end or fold it under and tie to equalize thickness. (Use this for Beef Stroganoff.) Have meat at room temperature and spread with butter. Insert meat thermometer in thickest part. Place filet in covered pit over glowing grey coals with a few chips of mesquite or hickory. Roast until meat thermometer reads 120 degrees for rare meat, 130 degrees for medium. Remove filet from heat and let stand 10 minutes before slicing thinly. Garnish with parsley and season with salt and pepper. It needs nothing else.

To Pack: Beef filet, butter, parsley, salt and pepper, barbeque equipment.

Apricot-Glazed Ham

1 medium Cure 81 or other
  quality boneless ham
1/4 pound dried apricots

1/2 gallon pineapple juice
  from dairy case

GLAZE

1 cup apricot preserves
1/4 cup orange juice
1 1/2 tablespoons Dijon mustard

1/4 teaspoon powdered cloves
1/4 teaspoon powdered ginger

At Home: In non-aluminum pot, dilute 1 1/2 quarts pineapple juice with enough water to barely cover ham. Bring to boil, then reduce heat and simmer 20 minutes. Let ham cool in marinade, then place in refrigerator overnight. Simmer apricots in 1 pint pineapple juice till just tender. Place in refrigerator.

Combine glaze ingredients and coat ham with half of glaze. Bake ham at 325 degrees for 15 minutes; remove and coat with remaining glaze for a final 15 minutes of baking. If ham begins to scorch, add a bit of the marinade in bottom of pan. Wrap ham tightly in foil; refrigerate.

To Pack: Ham, apricots and parsley.

In Camp: Serve ham on platter decorated with apricots and parsley.

Persian Eggplant

Simple and elegant. This recipe was the main course at a summer dinner party in Uptown New Orleans. Cheese, fruit, white wine, and coffee rounded out the menu.

2 medium eggplants
Salt and pepper
5 eggs

Butter
1 1/2 cups plain yogurt
4 tablespoons sesame seeds

At Home: Peel, chop, and steam eggplants until very tender. Salt and pepper to taste. Separate eggs; beat yolks well and whites stiff. Combine yolks with eggplant and fold in whites. Spread eggplant in buttered shallow baking pan and bake at 300 degrees until just set, about 25 minutes. When cool, spread eggplant with yogurt and sprinkle with sesame seeds. Wrap dish tightly with foil. Serve cold or hot.

To Pack: Eggplant dish.

In Camp: Serve cold from ice chest or steamed over hot water. Serves 4.

Summer / Mandeville Fourth of July

Cheese Board

Appetizers, lunches, even desserts all reach apotheosis in a carefully chosen board of ripe cheeses. Try one of these combinations or make up your own, a venture greatly enhanced by knowledgeable staff of a wine and cheese shop. And don't forget that all fruit, particularly pears, apples, and green, red, or black grapes enhance your cheese board.

Canadian Cheddar	Baby Swiss	Bucheron
Emmenthaler	Vermont Cheddar	Gorgonzola
Roquefort	Edam	Camembert
Brie	Saga	Cheshire

Jarlsberg and on and on...

At Home: Assemble cheeses and wrap tightly.

To Pack: Cheeses, crackers, knife, fruit, tray.

In Camp: Serve partially sliced cheeses on board or tray with assorted fruits and crackers.

Gail's Rum Cake

I wanted to include a made-from-scratch rum cake, but this was better.

1 cup chopped pecans or walnuts	4 large eggs
1 box good quality yellow cake mix	1/2 cup cold water
	1/2 cup dark rum (Myers is best)
1 (3-ounce) box vanilla pudding mix	1/2 cup oil

GLAZE

1/4 cup butter	1/2 cup sugar
1/4 cup water	1 cup dark rum

At Home: Sprinkle nuts on bottom of greased Bundt pan. Preheat oven to 325 degrees. Put ingredients in big bowl and beat with mixer according to cake package directions. Pour into pan and bake about 1 hour or until cake tests done.

Make glaze by combining ingredients and heating until sugar melts. Remove cake from pan and pour glaze over. Store cooled cake in cake tin.

To Pack: Cake in tin.

In Camp: Slice and smile. Makes 10-12 generous servings.

3

Red Creek Cool-Off:
A Mississippi Float Trip

Fierce sun, blue-blazing thunderstorms: August in the South is the cruelest month for campers. Even fanatical ones like us venture from our air-conditioned lairs reluctantly...unless we head for Red Creek.

We last canoed Red Creek in the sorry dog days of August, braving the heat in a desperate bid to shake cabin fever. In the aggressive glare of the noonday sun, we launched our boats and knew right away we were in trouble. Either we adapted fast or were sentenced to a two-day grilling between broiling sky and baking beaches. So we adapted.

Slithering into the current, we began what turned out to be a weekend belly-float behind the canoes. The creek did its part; swirling beneath the shade of oak and swamp maple, gliding past mossy banks trickling with springs—as long as we stayed wet, we

Catching a dragonfly while cooling off.

stayed cool. Equally pleasant, we found, was the cooter's-eye-view of life at water level. As a further adaptation to August, we'd left the camp stove at home: salads for lunch, salads for dinner, no cooking allowed. Which left more time for meetings of the Hippo Society, lengthy affairs where members chin-deep in creek water sipped tea by the quart, beer by the can, and even a drop or two of rosé at evening.

After two days of the amphibious life, comfortable in the worst of the southern summer, we returned, refreshed, to civilization, a place where air conditioners no longer seemed quite so necessary.

For information on canoeing Red Creek:

Mississippi Department of Wildlife Conservation
P. O. Box 451
Jackson, MS 39205
601/961-5300

MENUS
(*indicates recipes given)

Breakfast
Frizzled Ham*
Fresh Lemon Cake* • Honeydew Slices with Lime Wedges
Cold Coffee Eggnog*

Lunch
Traveling Salad Bar* • Cheese Wafers
Pepperidge Farm Hazelnut Cookies
Summer Tea*

Dinner
Mixed Nuts . Watermelon Pickle
Southern Chicken Salad* • Peppery Rice Salad*
Sliced Homegrown Tomatoes with Chopped Basil
Nectarines • Cherries • Bel Paese Cheese
Macaroons
Wine: A versatile Rosé like Buena Vista Blanc de Pinot Noir

Summer / Red Creek Cool-Off

Frizzled Ham

Thin-sliced ham Brown sugar
Powdered cloves Butter

At Home: Sprinkle ham with a hint of powdered cloves and more than a hint of brown sugar. Heat butter and fry ham briefly until frizzled. Transport in Ziploc freezer bag.

To Pack: Ham.   *In Camp:* Serve cold.

Fresh Lemon Cake

1 lemon 3/4 cup sugar
1 egg 1/2 cup milk
1 cup all-purpose flour 1/2 cup golden raisins
1/2 teaspoon salt 1/4 cup coarsely chopped
1/2 teaspoon baking soda   walnuts
1/4 cup butter

At Home: Grease small loaf pan (you can use a regular size one, but it will be only half full) and preheat oven to 350 degrees. Squeeze lemon and save juice. Remove lemon peel with potato peeler and whirr with egg in blender until smooth. Sift flour with salt and soda. Cream butter, gradually beating in sugar until fluffy. Add egg mixture. Stir in flour alternately with milk. Add raisins and walnuts. Bake 30 minutes or until golden brown and shrinking from pan sides. Sprinkle top with reserved lemon juice. When cool, remove, wrap in foil and freeze, if desired. Makes 1 small loaf; double recipe for a generous one.

To Pack: Lemon Cake.

In Camp: Serve on plate in thin slices.

Cold Coffee Eggnog

4 cups milk 2 tablespoons instant coffee
2 eggs 1 teaspoon vanilla
1/4 cup honey

At Home: Mix ingredients and beat till foamy. Strain into plastic jar. Refrigerate. Makes 4 cups.

To Pack: Eggnog.

In Camp: Serve cold. Or hot. A delicious way to pack extra protein.

Summer / Red Creek Cool-Off

Traveling Salad Bar

This is an elegant lunch, not too much trouble to set up for a special group. For the finished product, you'll have lightweight trays piled with:

Cottage Cheese Garden Salad
  (see recipe below)
Chunk light tuna
Grated carrot
Sliced boiled eggs
Radishes

Grated Cheddar
Sliced tomatoes
Sliced cucumbers
Black olives
Thousand and One Island
  Dressing

Cottage Cheese Garden Salad

2 cups creamed cottage cheese
1/4 bunch chopped parsley
2 carrots, finely chopped
1 stalk celery, finely chopped
1 small bell pepper,
  finely chopped

1 small cucumber, finely
  chopped
2 green onions, finely chopped
Salt, pepper, celery salt
Tabasco to taste

At Home: Combine ingredients; transport refrigerated in covered plastic bowl or container. Makes about 4 cups.

Thousand and One Island Dressing

1 cup Hellman's mayonnaise
Juice of 1 lemon
1 small clove garlic, minced
1 small garlic pickle, minced
1 teaspoon Worcestershire

1/4 cup catsup
1 green onion, minced
1 hardboiled egg, finely
  chopped

At Home: Combine ingredients: transport refrigerated in widemouth jar. Makes about 1 1/2 cups.

To Pack: Widemouth jar of dressing, plastic container of cottage cheese salad, can of tuna, Ziploc bags of: grated carrots, boiled eggs, radishes, romaine, grated Cheddar, tomatoes, cucumbers, olives.

In Camp: Arrange vegetables, tuna, eggs, and cheese on large tray around bowl of "Cottage Cheese Garden Salad." Serve with dressing.

Summer / Red Creek Cool-Off

Summer Tea

13 tea bags
1/4 cup fresh mint leaves, washed
1 quart water
Juice of 2 lemons

1 (6-ounce) can orange juice concentrate
1 cup sugar or to taste
Mint sprigs

At Home: Combine tea bags, mint leaves and 1 quart water. Cover, bring to boil, remove from heat, and steep 3 minutes. Add juices, sugar to taste and water to equal 2 quarts. Transport in insulated jug. Makes 2 quarts.

To Pack: Tea, fresh mint sprigs.

In Camp: Serve on ice garnished with fresh mint sprigs.

Southern Chicken Salad

Leftovers are good for lunch—on lettuce or in sandwiches.

1 (1-inch) piece fresh ginger root or 1 teaspoon ginger
1 teaspoon sage
Water
1 hen
1 cup chopped celery

3 hardboiled eggs, finely chopped
Mayonnaise to moisten
Juice of 1 lemon
Salt, pepper, and celery salt

At Home: Boil hen in water to cover to which you have added ginger and sage. When tender, remove meat and chop into small chunks. Mix with remaining ingredients. Keep very cold and transport in Ziploc freezer bags or plastic container.

To Pack: Chicken salad, lettuce for garnish (optional).

In Camp: Serve from tray garnished with lettuce or from plastic container. Makes about 10-12 servings.

Summer / Red Creek Cool-Off

Peppery Rice Salad

The contrast of the creamy chicken salad with a spicy rice salad is unexpected, pleasantly so.

2 bay leaves
Water
1 1/2 cups raw rice, cooked
4 stalks celery, chopped fine
3 tablespoons capers
1 medium green pepper,
  finely chopped
1 4-ounce jar pimientos,
  drained and chopped

5 green onions, finely chopped
3-4 tablespoons pepper vinegar
  (this is the hot stuff surround-
  ing jalapeno or birds-eye
  peppers in their jars)
Salt and pepper to taste
Chopped fresh parsley for
  garnish

At Home: Boil rice in water flavored with bay leaves. Drain and toss with remaining ingredients. Taste for seasoning, oil, and vinegar. Refrigerate till cool, then pack in Ziploc bag and return to refrigerator.

To Pack: Rice salad.

In Camp: Serve cool but not cold. Makes 6-8 servings.

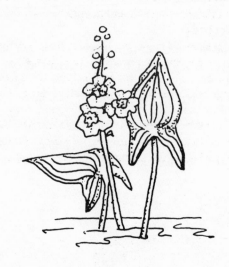

Summer / Red Creek Cool-Off

4

Coastal Camping in Maine:
Car Camping Far From Home

As long as our kitchens are near, we can all happily whip out fine camp meals with the *At Home/In Camp* method. But what happens when that kitchen is hundreds of airplane and rental car miles away, when we're camping far from home with only the kitchen gear stuffable into a square foot of backpack? As we proved on an August trip to Recompense Shore Campground on the rocky southern coast of Maine near Freeport, we can still eat well. All it takes is the right gear, some creative grocery shopping, and a spirit of adventure.

The Gear: What emerged from the bulging compartments of my backpack were (1) a one-burner propane stove minus propane canister (which can be bought virtually anywhere), (2) matches in a waterproof case, (3) a 10-inch folding skillet, (4) two lightweight nesting pots, (5) a half gallon lightweight thermal jug, (6) plastic cups, (7) camping forks and spoons, (8) a sharp knife, (9) a corkscrew, (10) a micro-bottle of detergent and a pot scrubber, (11) Ziploc bags containing salt and pepper, brown sugar, garlic, plus a few extra bags.

The Groceries: Next came the treasure hunt: scavenging for food. Not far from our bayside camp, we discovered the Bay Street Market where we filled our basket with fresh Maine potatoes (so good we could and did make a meal of them), sweet corn, Vermont Cheddar, and Red Rose brand tea, and, more mundanely, the crucial propane canister, heavy aluminum foil, heavy paper plates, and reams of paper towels. We drove on to the Freeport docks and picked up hot steamed lobsters in a paper bag, then

A hilltop view of the rocky Maine coastline and woods.

on to an organic beef farm near camp for succulent rib steaks sans chemical additives. (And dare I mention the few, very few clams we dug illegally a few yards from our tent?)

In other words we did a thorough job of unearthing the good stuff locally. And if shopping was fun, eating was more so; we sipped our Chardonnay and savored our clams and swooned over our lobsters in a state as close to nirvana as we'll ever get. All that and the blue-silk waters of Casco Bay.

For information on Maine camping:

Recompense Shore Campsites
Burnett Road
Freeport, Maine 04032
207/865-4469

Winter number for summer
reservations: 207/865-9307

L.L. Bean
Freeport, Maine 04032

Gear-freak's paradise
Open 24 hours a day.

MENUS

(*indicates recipes given)

Breakfast

Cranapple Juice
Thick-Sliced Bacon, Fried Country Eggs, and Skillet Toast*
Raspberry Jam
Red Rose Brand Tea

Lunch

Poacher's Sandwiches*
Garlic Pickles • Vermont Cheddar • Gravenstein Apples
Cold Milk

Dinner

Freeport Dock Steamed Lobsters
Buttered Maine Potatoes* • Fresh Corn in Foil*
Blueberries in Cream*
Wine: The best Chardonnay you can afford—try the delicious
moderately priced Navarro Mendocino

Thick-Sliced Bacon, Fried Country Eggs, and Skillet Toast

Thick-sliced bacon
Fresh country eggs

Bakery white bread, unsliced
Butter

In Camp: Fry bacon in skillet until crisp. Remove and drain on paper plate. Pour off most of the bacon drippings, and fry thick slices of bread until they are slightly crisp and heated through. Wrap in foil and put in a warm place if there is one. Fry eggs and transfer to sturdy paper plate with bacon and toast. For dessert, not that you need it, have another piece of bread, untoasted this time, with butter and raspberry jam. When you get home, get back on the oat bran.

Poacher's Sandwiches

I know, bad for the arteries, but once in your life?

2 tablespoons butter
3/4 pound rare leftover organic
  beef steak, sliced thin
Salt and pepper to taste
Squeeze of fresh lemon juice

4 slices leftover breakfast
  bacon
Bakery white bread or French
  bread

In Camp: Heat butter and add beef and seasonings; heat through. Remove beef to paper plate; add lemon juice to pan. Brush thick slices of bread with pan juices and layer with beef and bacon. Wrap sandwiches in foil and carry on a hike to neighboring Wolf Neck State Park. Serves 2.

Buttered Maine Potatoes

Fresh Maine potatoes
Butter

Salt and pepper

In Camp: I was astonished to discover the difference between regular store-bought potatoes and fresh Maine potatoes. They truly need no treatment other than scrubbing, dicing, quick boiling, and saucing with butter, salt and pepper. We could have skipped the lobster and still enjoyed a feast.

Fresh Corn in Foil

Corn   Salt and pepper
Butter

To Pack: Corn, salt, pepper and butter.

In Camp: Shuck corn and coat each ear with butter, salt, and
pepper. Wrap ears individually in 4x12-inch pieces of foil and
roast on grill over hot coals, turning corn for even cooking. Alternatively and more simply, you can shuck corn, break ears in half,
and cook about 5 minutes in water with potatoes. Serve with
plenty of butter, salt and pepper.

Blueberries and Cream

Small Maine blueberries   Brown sugar
Heavy cream

To Pack: Blueberries, cream, and sugar.

In Camp: Wash blueberries, drain on paper towels and serve au
natural with cream and brown sugar.

California Chardonnay

Buy yourself a fine bottle of Chardonnay and sip it reverently
from your lowly plastic cup as you watch the sun sink and the tide
return. Only when the sacramental bottle is empty should you
attack the lobster and company.

5

Deep Summer in the Felicianas:
Bicycle Exploring in Plantation Country

Summer lies more gently on the old, proud land of the Felicianas than it does on the rest of Louisiana. A few miles but many years from the urban life of Baton Rouge and New Orleans, these green and rolling parishes cut with steep, ferny ravines are a haven for anyone weary of summer.

Even on a sweltering day in July, the backroads of East and West Feliciana—narrow sunken traces winding nowhere and back—are pleasant places to bicycle. Randomly we pick a road heading any direction out of St. Francisville or Clinton or Jackson. A left turn, a right turn, and we just as randomly park the car and saddle up. We rarely know where we're headed, but not once have we been disappointed in what we've found.

Keeping cool in the damp heat is easy on a bicycle, for straining up hills raises a sweat that sailing down evaporates. Sometimes we cool off more thoroughly in a clear, sandy stream; Clark Creek, our favorite, is known not only for its 15-foot waterfalls, but for a priceless cache of Indian artifacts unearthed there a few years back. Exploring the Felicianas is exploring the past and often we'll come upon some lonely ghost house of the 1800's tucked away on one of the out-backest of the back roads. Down some cicada-thrumming live oak allee' we stumble on a Greenwood or an Ellerslie, an Asphodel or a Solitaire.

At night we camp on the wide sandy banks of Thompson Creek. We eat our twentieth century dinner, the ghosts recede and all that remains is a trail of stars, brightness the cities no longer see.

For information on bicycling in the Felicianas:

Louisiana Department of
Transportation
P. O. Box 44245
Baton Rouge, LA 70804
504/342-7849

Request parish maps for East and
West Feliciana.

Directions to Clark Creek Natural Area (just outside the Felicianas near Pond, Mississippi): Take U.S. 61 north of Baton Rouge to LA 66 (Angola Highway) north of St. Francisville at Bains. Turn left, drive about

A brief rest from summer cycling in the deep shade of the Felicianas.

12 miles and turn right at Pinckneyville, MS sign. Four miles beyond Pinckneyville is Pond, MS. Turn left at Clark Creek directional signs, drive 300 yards past Pond General Store and park. This road is itself good, if steep, bicycling.

MENUS

(*indicates recipes given)

Breakfast

Home-squeezed Orange Juice
Homemade Granola* and Bananas • Orange Nut Bread*
Iced Coffee with Brown Sugar and Cream

Lunch

Ploughman's Lunch*
Kentwood Spring Water

Dinner

St. Francisville Spinach Dip* • Corn Chips
Seashell Salad* • Carrot, Celery, and Pepper Sticks on Ice*
Cantaloupe and Watermelon Bowl
Pepperidge Farm Party Rolls
Lemon Cream Tarts*
Wine: Just for fun, try something bubbly, like a great bargain
bottle of Cadiz Brut Reserva

Homemade Granola

1 cup wheat germ
1 cup powdered milk
1 cup shredded coconut
1/4 cup oil
4 cups oatmeal
3 cups chopped pecans,
    walnuts, or almonds
1 cup sesame seeds

1 cup sunflower seeds
5 cups chopped dried fruit:
    peach, apple, fig, date,
    apricot, gold or dark raisins
1/2 cup honey
1/2 cup molasses
1/4 cup hot water

At Home: Stir wheat germ, powdered milk, coconut and oil together. Add oatmeal, nuts, sesame seeds, sunflower seeds, and fruit. Combine honey, molasses, and hot water, pour over fruit and mix together with hands. Spread 1/2 to 1-inch deep on baking sheet. Bake at 325 degrees for 1 hour or until crisp and golden brown, stirring every 5 minutes and *watch to prevent burning.* Do not overbake! Cool and pack in Ziploc freezer bags. Freeze, if you like. Makes about 4 quarts.

To Pack: Granola, milk, bananas.

In Camp: Serve with milk and sliced bananas. Don't forget the dental floss.

Orange Nut Bread

2 cups all-purpose flour	2 tablespoons lemon juice
1 tablespoon baking soda	1 tablespoon grated orange rind
3/4 teaspoon salt	1/4 teaspoon grated lemon rind
1/2 cup sugar	1/4 cup melted shortening
1 egg	3/4 cup broken pecan pieces
3/4 cup orange juice	

At Home: Sift flour with soda, salt and sugar. Combine beaten egg with orange juice, lemon juice, rinds, and melted shortening. Add dry ingredients, stirring till well mixed. Add nuts. Turn into well-greased and sugared bread tin. Cover and let stand 20 minutes. Bake at 350 degrees for 1 hour or until bread is browned and tests done. Cool, wrap in foil and freeze, if you like. Makes 1 loaf.

To Pack: Bread, butter, cream cheese.

In Camp: Warm and serve plain or with butter or cream cheese.

Ploughman's Lunch

Cheshire cheese	Bakery rolls and butter
Imported Gruyere cheese	Purple pickled onions
Herbed Cheese	

To Pack: Insulate cheeses and butter with foam or cloth covering; rolls, pickled onions, foil.

In Camp: Set out cheeses, rolls, and onions on foil. If this were other than a bicycling lunch, hot tea or cold beer would go down well.

Summer / Deep Summer in the Felicianas

St. Francisville Spinach Dip

Some campers have tried to get at this with a spoon.

1 (10-ounce) package frozen
  chopped spinach
1 (8-ounce) package cream
  cheese, cubed and softened
1/2 teaspoon Tabasco

6 slices bacon, cooked crisp
  and crumbled or 1/2 cup
  Baco-Bits
2 1/2 tablespoons lemon juice

At Home: Cook spinach and drain well. With electric mixer, beat cream cheese until creamy. Add spinach, Tabasco, and lemon juice and blend well. Top with bacon. Makes 1 pint.

To Pack: Dip, chips, vegetables.

In Camp: Serve with large corn chips or dipping vegetables.

Seashell Salad

16 ounces seashell pasta
2 cups boiled shrimp
4 tablespoons olive oil
4 tablespoons lemon juice
1/2 cup chopped green onions
1/2 cup chopped parsley
2 teaspoons fresh basil,
  snipped

1 cup whole pitted
  black olives
2 cups fresh blanched
  green beans
2 cups thinly-sliced
  celery
1 cup sliced radishes
Salt and pepper

At Home: Cook pasta in boiling well-salted water until just tender. Do not overcook. Combine remaining ingredients and toss gently. Taste for seasoning. Transport in plastic container.

Note: As you probably know, almost anything tastes good with good pasta, so you can use your discretion to add or subtract ingredients.

To Pack: Salad, lettuce, relishes.

In Camp: Serve from container or place on a tray with lettuce and relishes. Serves 4-6.

Carrot, Celery, and Pepper Sticks on Ice

At Home: Cut vegetables into sticks, put in Ziploc bags with a squeeze of lemon and refrigerate.

To Pack: Vegetables, large plastic glass.

In Camp: Half fill a large plastic glass with ice and arrange the vegetable sticks in a sort of stiff bouquet on top... attractive way to keep vegetables cold and crisp.

Lemon Cream Tarts

These are sometimes called "Lemon Curd Tarts". Whatever you call them, be sure to top them with sour cream. They're extravagantly good.

1 stick butter	6 beaten eggs
3/4 cup fresh lemon juice	Baked tart shells
1 tablespoon grated lemon rind	Sour cream
1 1/2 cup sugar	

At Home: Blend first 5 ingredients and cook in double boiler, whisking till thick and smooth. This takes a while. Chill filling in plastic container. Bake frozen shells and transport in oatmeal box or plastic container.

To Pack: Filling, tart shells, sour cream.

In Camp: Spoon filling into baked shells and top with sour cream. The filling keeps for several days, refrigerated. Makes 12 small tarts.

Toddlers aren't much help in the kitchen, but they're good and cheerful campers all the same.

6

Summer Day at Shining Rock:
A North Carolina Family Wilderness Excursion

Wilderness camping is for backpackers. Only they, unbowed by the weight of a 70-pound pack and undaunted by the prospect of freeze-dried turkey a' la king, are tough enough to ramble in vast, untrammeled lands devoid of picnic tables. At least that was the warped notion that prevailed in me before Laurie and Dr. John, the North Carolina camping connection, presented us with an alternative known as wilderness camping for wimps.

Asheville was simmering in a July heat wave as John's over-stuffed Aerostar humped up the Blue Ridge Parkway headed for the 13,000 acres of Shining Rock Wilderness less than an hour away. Four adults, teen-aged Caroline, toddler Kit, tons of gear, and chests of glamorous food—we were a motley and far from spartan crew. Nevertheless, we too were wilderness-bound. The plan was simple: park the van at the Big East Fork Trailhead, load up the gear, and lug it only as far as the first good campsite. Which didn't take long; once we reached the Pigeon River, everywhere-looked good and virtually no one else was around.

Without delay, we made camp in a clearing overlooking a four-foot waterfall. The pool at the bottom, see-through aqua to its sandy floor, petals of shellpink rosebay floating on its limpid surface, was irresistible. Stripping as far as modesty allowed, we plunged like overheated summer polar bears into the glacial foam churning below the falls. Ten minutes later we shimmied onto the warm rocks, beautifully chilled, to drip-dry in the sun. The came lunch.

Maybe with just a quarter-mile hike we hadn't actually earned our wilderness. But there at Shining Rock, undeserving or no, we had it all—rosebay in bloom, mood-elevating falls, and food that backpackers could only dream of.

For information on Shining Rock Wilderness:

Supervisor's Office
National Forests in North Carolina
P. O. Box 2750
Asheville, NC 28802
704/257-4200

Permits are required for camping.

MENUS

(*indicates recipes given)

Breakfast

Creole Lost Bread* • Miniature Smoked Sausages
Creole Cream Cheese and Fruit*
Cafe au Lait

Lunch

Antipasto Al Fresco*
White Sangria* or Ice Water

Dinner

Peppers Provencal* • Italian Bread
Cold Lemon Chicken* • Barbecued Italian Sausage*
Pesto*
Italian Cheese Board*
European Summer Fruit*
Wine: A pear-tasting Italian wine like Ruffino Libaio
Cappuccino*

Creole Lost Bread

5 eggs
1/2 cup milk
1/4 teaspoon grated orange
  peel
1/4 teaspoon grated lemon
  peel
1/2 cup sugar

1 large loaf stale French bread
  sliced 1/2-inch thick
1 stick butter
2 tablespoons oil
Powdered sugar and nutmeg,
  or cane syrup or honey

At Home: Beat eggs well, add milk, grated peel, and sugar. Transport in jar.

To Pack: Egg mixture, bread, butter, oil, powdered sugar and nutmeg, or syrup, or honey.

In Camp: Cut bread and, using a pot or platter for batter, dip bread on both sides. Fry bread until golden in hot butter and oil. Serve hot with powdered sugar and nutmeg, or cane syrup, or honey. Serves 6.

Summer / Summer Day at Shining Rock

Creole Cream Cheese and Fruit

Serve this after the lost bread and sausages have gone down, as a sort of dessert. Remember, these are meals to linger over while you're pumping Brother Big John about how and *why* to catch alligator gar or discovering what Sister Pat really thought of Earl the Pearl in the 10th grade.

Creole cream cheese (or large   Bananas
   curd cottage cheese saturated   Plums
   with heavy cream)   Strawberries
Fresh peaches

To Pack: Creole cream cheese, fruit.

In Camp: Arrange the fruit artistically, cut up, on a tray and center it with a bowl of Creole cream cheese.

Antipasto Al Fresco

Antipasto is a grand starter for an Italian meal, but few realize what a marvelous lunch it can be. This one is authentic and thoroughly sensuous, a blend of opposites—sweet and salty, crisp and tender, dark and light. First I'll tell you how it ends up, then give recipes for starting it off.

To Pack and In Camp: On three trays or pizza pans, arrange the following.

   1. Large black Alfonso olives. Large bronze Calabrese olives. Small green Italian pickled peppers. Two-inch long, thick-cut celery sticks. Small quartered home-grown tomatoes. Thin crescent slices of cantaloupe.

   2. Paper-thin slices of Genoa salami. Anchovy fillets. Smoked Provolone cheese. Fontina cheese. Italian bread sticks. Green onions.

   3. Special Italian Salad. Caponata. Halved hardboiled eggs

Summer / Summer Day at Shining Rock

Special Italian Salad

1 small head green cabbage,
  grated or finely chopped
1 bunch flat-leaf Italian
  parsley, chopped
2 stalks bright green celery,
  finely chopped

1/2 cup Sicilian green olives
1 small jar pimiento
Olive oil to moisten
Salt and freshly-ground black
  pepper to taste
1 can albacore tuna, drained

At Home: Mix all ingredients but tuna and transport in plastic container or Ziploc freezer bags.

To Pack: Salad and tuna, can opener.

In Camp: Flake tuna and blend gently into salad. Although this salad is not as dramatic without the tuna, it is refreshing and pairs well with grilled Italian sausage or chicken for dinner. Serves 6-8.

Caponata

1/2 cup olive oil
2 cups minced celery
3/4 cup minced onion
2 pounds eggplant, peeled
  and cubed (about 8 cups)
Salt to taste
1/3 cup wine vinegar
3 cups Italian plum tomatoes,
  drained

2 tablespoons tomato paste
1 tablespoon minced garlic
6 large green olives, slivered
2 tablespoons capers
4 anchovy fillets, mashed
  to paste
Freshly-ground pepper
4 teaspoons sugar

At Home: Fry celery and onion in 1/4 cup olive oil for 10 minutes. Remove from pan, add 1/4 cup olive oil and saute eggplant on high until light brown. Return celery and onion to skillet and stir in rest of ingredients. Bring to boil, reduce heat and simmer 15 minutes. Taste for seasoning and vinegar. Chill and transport in covered plastic container or Ziploc freezer bags.

To Pack: Caponata.

In Camp: Serve cool but not cold. Serves 6-8.

White Sangria

1 quart Chablis or other
  white wine
2 tablespoons lemon juice
2 tablespoons orange juice

1 quart club soda
Slices of orange, lemon,
  and lime

At Home: Mix wine, juices and fruit slices, chill and carry in
thermos.

To Pack: Wine mixture, club soda.

In Camp: Mix chilled club soda half and half with wine mixture.
Any red or white wine can be used to make this wonderfully quaf-
fable hot-weather drink. Serves 8.

Peppers Provencal

1/4 cup olive oil
1 red pepper, sliced thin
1 green pepper, sliced thin
Pinch each of thyme, oregano,
  rosemary, and basil

Salt and freshly ground pepper
  to taste
2 medium onions, sliced thin
3 garlic cloves, minced

At Home: Saute peppers and seasonings except garlic in oil on
low heat for 10 minutes, then add onions and saute until vegetables are tender. You may need to add a tablespoon or so of
water during this time. During last 5 minutes of cooking, add
garlic. Makes about 2 cups.

To Pack: Peppers Provencal, Italian bread.

In Camp: Serve on slices of Italian bread. These peppers are
delicious on lots of other things like crackers, boiled potatoes, or
scrambled eggs, to name a few.

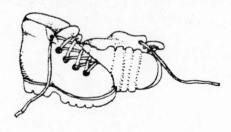

Cold Lemon Chicken

5 pounds frying chicken parts,
skinned
1 cup fresh lemon juice
1 tablespoon grated lemon peel
2 tablespoons brown sugar

2 cups flour
2 teaspoons salt
1 teaspoon pepper
1/2 cup oil
2 lemons, sliced thin

At Home: Marinate chicken overnight in lemon juice, lemon peel, and brown sugar.

Combine flour, salt and pepper in a paper bag and coat chicken well. Saute chicken in oil until golden. Preheat oven to 350 degrees as you arrange chicken in single layer in baking dish and add leftover marinade to bottom. If marinade does not cover bottom of dish, add a little water or lemon juice. Bake chicken, turning once, for 1/2 hour or until tender.

Top each chicken piece with one or more slices of lemon; chill, and transport in plastic container.

To Pack: Lemon Chicken, lemon.

In Camp: Pile chicken on a platter garnished with fresh lemon slices. Be sure to sample a piece to test for seasoning. Serves 8-10.

Barbecued Italian Sausage

Since Italian sausages are notoriously thin-skinned, it's a good idea to gently parboil them at home after pricking them all over with a fork. This firms them up for a final finish on the grill.

Pesto

Basil practically grows itself, so there's no excuse not to fling a handful of seeds at your garden. If you've never tasted Pesto, it's impossible to imagine how good it is.

1 pound linguini
Large pot of salted water

1 cup Pesto Sauce

Pesto Sauce

1 cup fresh basil leaves,
  washed and dried
2 large garlic cloves, minced
1/2 cup walnuts or pecans

1/2 cup olive oil
1/2 cup freshly grated Parmesan or Romano cheese
Salt and pepper to taste

At Home: Combine basil, garlic, and nuts in blender and chop. Add olive oil slowly until blended. Add cheese, salt and pepper and blend briefly. Transport in jar.

To Pack: Linguini, salt, water, Pesto sauce, pot strainer.

In Camp: Bring water to boil, covered. Add linguini and cook till barely tender. Drain with pot-drainer. Toss immediately and thoroughly with Pesto Sauce and serve hot or at air temperature. If ice chest space is no object, prepare the pestoed pasta at home and serve it cold, sprinkled with extra grated cheese. Serves 4-6.

Italian Cheese Board

On your ever-handy lightweight tray, lay out a selection of red grapes, crackers and:

Fontina (left over from lunch)
Smoked Provolone (likewise)
Gorgonzola

Asiago
Bel Paese

European Summer Fruit

A pot of cold water, a bobbing flotilla of such choice soft, summer fruits as peaches, plums, cherries, nectarines, and grapes, and your family can talk on half the night, possibly egged on by cups of tongue-loosening Cappuccino.

Note: Have you ever wanted to launch a campaign against grocery stores selling beauteous but underripe fruit that slowly ripens into decay, somehow skipping that critical edible middle stage? Protest! Then find a good farmer's market or produce stand and never, never buy fruit that doesn't smell good!

Cappuccino

Here's a sure-fire boon to conversation, (just make sure no one tapes it).

For each serving:

1 ounce cocoa mix
  (individual packet)
1 ounce cognac

6 ounces hot coffee
1 tablespoon whipped or
  unwhipped heavy cream

At Home: Make coffee. Transport in glass juice container.

To Pack: Cocoa mix, cognac, coffee, cream.

In Camp: Add cognac to cocoa mix in large insulated cup. Fill cup with hot coffee. Stir well and top with cream. Makes 1 serving.

Fall

Rising fog shrouds an early morning paddle.

1

Clear Springs Potluck:
Multi-Family Group Camping

If you were the kind of child who never got enough of the outdoors, and if your own kids take after you, why not make up for it with a glorious fall weekend camping together at Clear Springs Recreation Area near Meadville, Mississippi? A quiet lake, a clear, sandy-bottom stream, trails through bright-leaved hardwoods, and campsites hung on a hillside make togetherness at Clear Springs a pleasure rather than a burden. There's even a rustic picnic shelter, perfect for a communal potluck dinner. So why not extend the togetherness and invite several other families to join you?

The last time we camped at Clear Springs, our group numbered 22—two fat toddlers, ten teens, and ten cooks—exactly the right number to guarantee a sumptuous, virtually painless feast in the previously staked-out shelter. For all of us, it has remained a time to remember and one to re-live on at least one bright blue fall weekend a year.

For more information on Clear Springs:

National Forests in Mississippi
1001 W. Capitol Street, Suite 1141
Jackson, MS 39269
601/965-4391

Bude Ranger District
U.S. Forest Service
Highway 1
Meadville, MS 39653
601/384-5876

MENUS

(* indicates recipes given)

Breakfast

Grape Juice
One-Skillet Breakfast*
Bagels, Cream Cheese, and Orange Marmalade
Coffee • Milk for Kids

Lunch

Country Corn Chowder*
Garlic Pickles • Red Delicious Apples
Mississippi Tea Cakes*
Hot Prince of Wales Tea • Natural Flavor Soft Drinks for Kids

Dinner

Cheese and Wine Tasting Table*
Barbequed Stuffed Pork Chops*
Savory Sour Cream Meat Balls*
Elaine Fields' Crowd-Pleasing Lentils* • Rice Sautina*
Fresh Green Beans and Okra* • Cucumber Relish*
Fall Fruit Plate* • Old South Pound Cake*
Ice Chest of Soft Drinks

One-Skillet Breakfast

Kids love this.

1/2 pound lean bacon, chopped	1 cup or generous handful
12 large eggs, slightly	Cheddar cheese
beaten	Salt and pepper

To Pack: Bacon, eggs, cheese, salt and pepper.

In Camp: Fry bacon and drain off fat. (Or fry bacon at home and carry to camp in Ziploc bag.) Add slightly beaten eggs and cheese to crumbled drained bacon. Cook very slowly till the eggs are set and the cheese melted, stirring as little as possible. Serves 6-8.

Country Corn Chowder

1 cup chopped salt pork
2 medium onions,
  coarsely cut
1 tablespoon green pepper
  minced (optional)
2 cups whole milk

2 medium potatoes, partially
  boiled and cut up
1 (16-ounce) can creamed
  corn
Salt and pepper

At Home: Fry salt pork in skillet until crisp and brown. Drain fat and add onions and green pepper; cook 5 minutes on low. Add potatoes, milk, creamed corn and seasonings, then cook slowly for about 20 minutes. Carry to camp in widemouth jar or plastic container.

To Pack: Chowder and butter.

In Camp: Heat chowder slowly and top with butter. Serves 2-4.

Mississippi Tea Cakes

Good plain cookies, perfect with sweet tea.

1 stick soft butter
1 cup sugar
2 eggs, beaten
1 1/2 cups all-purpose flour
1 1/2 teaspoons baking
  powder

1/4 teaspoon salt
1/4 teaspoon cinnamon
1 tablespoon milk
1 1/2 teaspoons vanilla
1/2 cup ground pecans,
  ground in blender

At Home: Mix ingredients in order, beating with electric mixer until well-blended. Drop by teaspoonfuls on greased cookie sheet. Bake at 350 degrees for 10-12 minutes till pale golden. Pack in tin or oatmeal box. Makes about 3 dozen.

To Pack: Tea cakes.

In Camp: Serve with hot tea.

Fall / Clear Springs Potluck

Cheese and Wine Tasting Table

Cover your picnic table with the proverbial red and white checked cloth, preferably the plastic disposable kind that comes on a roll. Ask each family to bring a favorite wine (I'd pick any of the Avia wines—decent and very inexpensive), an interesting cheese, and something to serve it on, crackers or bread. Have a cooler of softdrinks for the kids. Do remember the corkscrew.

Barbequed Stuffed Pork Chops

Double, triple, or quadruple this recipe if necessary.

4 tablespoons butter
1/2 medium green pepper, minced
1 small onion, grated
1/4 teaspoon minced garlic
1/2 cup fresh or canned mushrooms, chopped
1 1/2 cups dry bread, torn in small pieces
1 egg, beaten
1/4 teaspoon thyme
1/2 teaspoon pepper
1/2 salt or to taste
Pinch cayenne
1/4 teaspoon garlic powder
2 cups chicken broth
4 tablespoons oil
6 (1-inch thick) center loin pork chops, trimmed, and with pocket cut (ask butcher to do this)

At Home: Saute vegetables in butter until soft. Add bread, beaten egg, seasonings, and 1/2 cup broth. Cook mixture until blended and soft. Using a teaspoon, pack stuffing loosely into chops and secure with twine or toothpicks. Brown stuffed chops in oil and place in single layer in baking pan; add remaining broth. Bake chops till tender in 300-degree oven about 1 hour, turning once. Add more broth if necessary. Cool and wrap chops individually in heavy foil. Refrigerate or freeze.

To Pack: Pork chops, tongs, grill or steamer.

In Camp: Heat thawed foil-wrapped chops on grill over coals until they are heated through; unwrap for final minute or two for a barbeque taste. Or you may heat foil-wrapped chops on top of steamer. Serves 6.

Savory Sour Cream Meat Balls

2 pounds lean ground beef
1 cup bread crumbs or
    wheat germ
1/2 cup grated onion
1 egg

1/2 cup water
1/2 teaspoon pepper
1 teaspoon salt
1 tablespoon prepared yellow
    mustard

SOUR CREAM SAUCE

6 tablespoons butter
2 cups water
2 beef cubes
4 tablespoons flour

1 1/2 cups sour cream
1/2 teaspoon salt or to taste
1 teaspoon dillweed

At Home: Mix meatball ingredients with hands until well blended. Form into golfball-size meatballs, dredge with flour, and place on cookie sheet. Bake in 450-degree oven until browned. Mix butter, water, beef cubes, and flour and cook until thick. Add remaining ingredients and heat briefly. Add meatballs to sauce. Refrigerate or freeze in widemouth jars or plastic containers.

To Pack: Meatballs in sauce, milk.

In Camp: Gently heat meatballs in sauce in pot or skillet until piping hot, adding a little water or milk if sauce is too thick. Serves 6-8.

Courtesy U.S. Forest Service (Mississippi).

Tall pines frame the rustic Clear Springs picnic shelter.

Elaine Fields' Crowd-Pleasing Lentils

Discover why my mother-in-law is the best cook in Opelousas, Louisiana.

1 pound lentils
8 cups water
1 bay leaf
3 cloves garlic, minced
Small green pepper, chopped
1 pound smoked pork sausage of excellent quality

1 pound "green" (unsmoked) sausage of excellent quality
2 cups chopped onions
1 (10-ounce) can whole tomatoes
Salt, pepper, cayenne

At Home: Place lentils in pot, cover with 8 cups water. Add bay leaf, garlic, and green pepper, and simmer 1/2 hour. Cut sausage in large pieces and fry in skillet until brown. Drain excess grease. Remove sausage and fry onions and drained tomatoes (save juice) until onions are clear and tomato is orange. Add tomato juice, sausage, and vegetables to lentils and simmer for about 45 minutes or until lentils are soft but not mushy. Season to taste with salt, pepper, and cayenne, and adjust liquid (lentils should be slightly soupy). Refrigerate or freeze when cool in Ziploc freezer bags.

To Pack: Lentils, Sierra cup ladle.

In Camp: Serve hot with Rice Sautina or Boiled Rice. Makes 4-6 servings.

Rice Sautina

The lentils and meatballs create wonderful combinations with this delicious rice.

1 stick butter
2 cups rice
4 cups chicken stock
2 tablespoons Kikkoman soy sauce

1/2 teaspoon salt
6 pieces bacon, cooked crisp and chopped, fat reserved
2/3 cup onions, chopped

At Home or In Camp: Melt butter in large pot and add rice; cook 3 minutes. Add chicken stock, soy sauce, and salt, and bring to boil. Simmer covered, 20 minutes. Cook onion in bacon fat until soft, then add bacon and onion to rice and fluff it up. Refrigerate or freeze in Ziploc freezer bag.

To Pack: Rice Sautina, butter.

In Camp: Re-heat with a little water and butter. Serves 6-8.

Fall / Clear Springs Potluck

Fresh Green Beans and Okra

Fresh young green beans   Butter
Fresh young okra   Salt and pepper

At Home or In Camp: Separately parboil beans and okra till tender-crisp. Add butter and carry to camp in plastic bags if precooking at home.

To Pack: Green beans and okra, salt and pepper.

In Camp: Put beans in pot with butter and a small amount of water. Top with okra and cook gently, covered, until both vegetables are just tender. Shake pot and season with salt and pepper.

Cucumber Relish

Chop fresh cucumbers, mild white onions, and sweet red peppers, and pack in a pint mason jar with Van Holten garlic pickle juice.

Fall Fruit Plate

Honeydew melon   Red raspberries
Peaches   Pears
Blue plums   Leaf Lettuce

DRESSING

Lime juice   Honey

At Home: Make dressing, using equal parts fresh lime juice and honey. Carry to camp in jar.

To Pack: Fruit, lettuce, dressing, tray, tongs.

In Camp: Line a lightweight tray with leaf lettuce. Arrange wedges of honeydew fan-shaped at two ends of platter. Then arrange peeled peach halves, dipped in dressing, cut side up. Arrange plum quarters between melon wedges. Arrange pear slices among peach halves. Pile raspberries in center. Serve dressing on the side.

Old South Pound Cake

Proud, elegant dowager of a cake, rich with flavor.

8 large eggs, separated
6 tablespoons sugar
1 pound butter (not margarine)
2 3/4 cups sugar

3 1/2 cups sifted
  all-purpose flour
1/2 cup half-and-half
1 tablespoon pure vanilla

At Home: Separate eggs and beat whites stiff, adding sugar toward end of beating. Place beaten egg whites in refrigerator.

Cream butter and sugar until blended and fluffy; add egg yolks and vanilla and beat well. Alternate flour and half-and-half. Fold in stiffly beaten egg whites. Bake in a buttered and sugared tube pan for about an hour and a half in a 325-degree oven. Carry to camp in cake tin. Sufficient for about 12 cake fanciers.

To Pack: Cake.

In Camp: Serve in hefty wedges. Sufficient for about 12 cake fanciers.

Fall / Clear Springs Potluck

2

Paddling the Piney:
Fall Color and Arkansas Whitewater

If you are bold enough to steal an unconventional four-day week-end in the Arkansas Ozarks during late October or early November, you may be lucky enough to find the milky green waters of Big Piney Creek splashing along unseasonably high beneath a psychedelic canopy of purple, red, and gold. When that happens, the mild guilt induced by knowledge of children, pets, and duty left behind will evaporate, instantly replaced by the joy of knowing you are in exactly the right place at precisely the right time.

That sense of being in the right place is enhanced if you camp at Long Pool Recreation Area off State Highway 7 north of Dover. Here the Big Piney has carved a horseshoe-shaped pool below bluffs where the few heavily wooded campsites perch. From here you can shuttle upstream for a pleasantly remote, mildly challenging day's paddle, ending the trip 500 feet from your picnic table. Next morning you can put in at the place you took out, paddle to Moore Outdoors or below, and have them shuttle you painlessly home again.

If convenience is the tone of Big Piney canoeing, it was reflected, too, in the food I brought on a recent trip for eight. Since I prepared dishes one by one over several weeks, the day before we left, I had nothing to do but shop for fresh food and unstash jars from the freezer.

For more information on the Big Piney:

Moore Outdoors
  Big Piney Creek Outpost
Hwy 164W at Twin Bridges
Rt. 2 Box 303 M
Dover, AR 72837
501/331-3606

Shuttles, rentals, river informa-.
tion.

Ozark Society Inc.
P.O. Box 2914
Little Rock, AR 72670

Information on streams, trails
and natural history.

An invigorating paddle in the splendor of Autumn.

MENUS

(* indicates recipes given)

Breakfast

Mexican Oranges*
Huevos Rancheros*
Beans with Chili and Chaurice*
Coffee

Lunch

Bavarian Meat Loaf Sandwiches*
Carrot Sticks
Polish Garlic Pickles (Van Holten's in plastic pack)
Hot Chocolate

Dinner

Hot Black Tea
Fresh Corn and Shrimp Stew*
Green Salad with Walnut Dressing*
Bakery Snowflake Rolls
Old-Fashioned Peanut Butter Cake*

Mexican Oranges

6 sweet, seedless oranges   6 tablespoons confectioner's
Cinnamon   sugar

At Home: Combine confectioner's sugar and cinnamon and transport in plastic bag.

To Pack: Oranges, sugar/cinnamon mixture.

In Camp: Peel and slice oranges, arrange on plate, and dust with sugar mixture. Serves 8-10.

Huevos Rancheros

Heats your insides, clears your sinuses, and tastes so good on a cold morning.

6 tablespoons chopped onion
2 cloves garlic, minced
4 tablespoons butter
1/4 cup chopped green pepper
4 tablespoons chopped jalapeno pepper, fresh or canned
1/2 teaspoon oregano
1/2 teaspoon cumin
2 large tomatoes, chopped
Salt and pepper
1 cup meat stock or tomato juice
8 large fresh eggs

At Home: Cook onion and garlic in butter till golden. Add peppers, oregano, cumin, tomato, salt, pepper, meat stock or tomato juice, and simmer until vegetables are tender and sauce thick. Carry to camp in Ziploc freezer bag, frozen, if you like.

To Pack: Frozen sauce bag, 8 eggs, large covered skillet.

In Camp: Heat sauce in large skillet. Add eggs, cover, and poach till whites are set. Huevos Rancheros are good with Cheese Grits and the sauce is good on scrambled eggs, too. Serves 8.

Beans with Chili and Chaurice

1 pound red kidney beans
1 pound pinto beans
2 bay leaves
2 medium onions, chopped
1/4 pound bacon, cut up
4 cloves garlic, minced
1 teaspoon thyme
3 tablespoons chili powder or to taste
3 tablespoons chopped fresh or pickled jalapenos
1 tablespoon salt
1 teaspoon garlic powder
1 large tomato, chopped
1 pound chaurice or andouille sausage, sliced thin
1 teaspoon cumin or to taste

At Home: Soak beans overnight. Drain and add water to reach 2 inches above beans. Add remaining ingredients and cook till tender, adding more water if necessary and stirring occasionally to prevent burning. When beans are tender but not mushy, cool and freeze in Ziploc freezer bags. Makes 12 cups.

To Pack: Beans.

In Camp: Serve with Huevos Rancheros. These are also good for a supper dish, served with rice, chopped onion and sour cream or with Fresh Vegetable Relish.

Fall / Paddling the Piney

Bavarian Meat Loaf Sandwiches

2 slices whole wheat bread,
   broken in small pieces
1/2 cup milk
2 pounds ground chuck (or
   veal or pork in various
   combination)
1 teaspoon minced garlic
1 medium onion, grated
2 tablespoons wheat germ
1/2 cup ground roasted nuts
   (pecans, cashews, walnuts)

2 eggs. beatem
1 teaspoon salt
1/2 teaspoon black pepper
1/2 teaspoon basil
1 tablespoon Worcestershire
Rye bread
Mayonnaise
Red leaf lettuce
Pickled beet slices
Mild onions

At Home: Soak bread in milk for 5 minutes, then mix with other ingredients. Pack firmly in loaf pan and bake at 300 degrees for 1 hour or until top is browned. Drain off excess fat and wrap pan in heavy foil. Refrigerate or freeze.

To Pack: Meat loaf, rye bread, mayonnaise, red leaf lettuce, pickled beet slices, and mild onions.

In Camp: Slice meat loaf and serve on fresh rye with mayonnaise, red lettuce, pickled beet slices, and onions.
Makes 10-12 sandwiches.

Fresh Corn and Shrimp Stew

This is at its peak freshly made, but still fine if made a day ahead; otherwise freeze it. Use only the freshest vegetables and shrimp.

1/4 cup flour
1/4 cup oil
1 cup each of chopped onion, green onion, and celery
3 quarts hot water
2 dozen ears of corn, cut whole kernel or 3 (10-ounce) packages frozen
1 cup diced fresh tomato

1/4 cup chopped parsley
2 cups fresh butter or lima beans
4 medium potatoes, cubed
Salt, pepper, and cayenne to taste
2 pounds fresh medium shrimp, peeled

At Home: Make a roux of the flour and oil and brown it lightly. Add onion, green onion, and celery and cook until onion is clear. Add hot water and remaining ingredients except for shrimp and simmer until vegetables are just tender, about 25 minutes. Add shrimp and cook till pink, about 5 minutes. Cool quickly and refrigerate in Ziploc freezer bags.

To Pack: Stew, butter.

In Camp: Serve hot with a pat of butter on top of each serving. Serves 8.

Green Salad with Walnut Dressing

Walnut oil is expensive, but distinctive. Make sure it's fresh when you buy it and keep it refrigerated.

Red leaf lettuce
Salad bowl lettuce

Chopped roasted walnuts

WALNUT DRESSING

2 tablespoons Dijon mustard
3 tablespoons red wine vinegar
7 tablespoons walnut oil

1/2 tablespoon minced parsley
Salt and fresh pepper

At Home: Whisk together the mustard and vinegar, then add oil and parsley and blend. Season to taste with salt and pepper, and carry to camp in jar.

To Pack: Washed, drained lettuces, walnuts, dressing, tongs.

In Camp: Tear lettuce, toss with Walnut Dressing, and sprinkle salad with chopped walnuts.

Old-Fashioned Peanut Butter Cake

This cake is luscious and simple to make.

1/2 stick butter
3/4 cup sugar
5 tablespoons crunchy
  peanut butter
1 large egg
1 1/3 cups all-purpose flour

1 teaspoon baking powder
1 teaspoon baking soda
1 cup buttermilk
  (have you tried the
  powdered mix)
1 teaspoon vanilla

ICING

3 ounces unsweetened chocolate
3 tablespoons butter
2 cups sifted
  confectioner's sugar
1/3 cup heavy cream

1 teaspoon vanilla
1/2 cup apricot preserves
  (optional)
2 tablespoons brandy
  (optional)

At Home: Preheat oven to 350 degrees and butter and sugar a 9-inch round cake pan. In large bowl, cream butter, sugar, and peanut butter; add egg. Measure flour, baking powder and baking soda, and sift. Add flour mixture alternately in thirds with buttermilk, beating after each addition. Add vanilla. Bake for 35-40 minutes or until cake tests done.

Icing: In heavy pan, melt chocolate and butter, stirring. Add sifted confectioners' sugar and cream and cook gently over very low heat, stirring constantly till blended and smooth. Stir in vanilla. At this point, you may (a) ice cake with chocolate icing or (b) split cake horizontally and spread bottom layer with warmed apricot jam combined with brandy, then replace layers and ice with chocolate icing. Carry to camp in cake tin and keep it cool.

To Pack: Cake.

In Camp: Serves about 6—stylishly.

Fall / Paddling the Piney

3

Down From Cloud Crossing:
Fishing and Wildlife-Watching on a
Louisiana Bayou

Cutting a tortuous route through the wet, dark heart of northern Louisiana's Kisatchie National Forest, Saline Bayou offers photographers and other watchers of wildlife passage into a fecund hardwood bottomland bursting with life. Canoes mark the outer limits of navigation, so you'll see few others floating the twisty shallow channel. If the water is high enough for October paddling, perhaps you'll meet a hunter or two, but if human life is scarce, wildlife is all around. By day, the great columns of cypress are alive with bird calls, and the mud beneath them tracked with the latent presence of deer and raccoon and wading birds; by

Photo by Hulin Robert.

A solitary canoe moves through the silent water of Saline Bayou.

night, the misty woods ring with the cries of barred owls.

Launch point for the journey into this wild land is the pleasantly primitive Cloud Crossing Campground, conveniently situated at the put-in point for a leisurely overnight paddle to the forest road near Goldonna. If you camp at Cloud Crossing on a Friday night and put in the water soon after breakfast on Saturday, you'll have plenty of time for photographing, bird watching, plant identification, and (in the case of the lone *practical* naturalist on our recent trip) fishing for your dinner.

For more information on Saline Bayou:

Supervisor's Office
Kisatchie National Forest
2500 Shreveport Highway
Pineville, LA 71360
318/473-7123

Maps of the Kisatchie National Forest and Cloud Crossing Recreation Area.

MENUS
(* indicates recipes given)

Breakfast
Grapefruit Halves
Denise's Creamy Turkey Hash*
Hot Raisin Bread and Butter
Coffee

Lunch
Natchitoches Meat Pies*
Golden Delicious Apples • Katy's Pralines*
Spiced Tea*

Dinner
Almond Butter on Wheat Crackers*
Portuguese Green Salad*
Pack and Paddle Courtbouillon* • Boiled Rice
Hot French Bread with Lagniappe*
Chocolate Ice Chest Pudding*
Coffee • Beer

Denise's Creamy Turkey Hash

Good on toast or grits, this stands well on its own—just bring enough.

2 tablespoons all-purpose flour
2 tablespoons butter
1 1/2 cups turkey broth
4 cups cubed white and dark
  turkey meat

1/2 cup heavy cream
Salt and pepper

At Home: Mix flour and butter and gradually add turkey broth, whisking till smooth. Add turkey meat and cook gently about 10 minutes. Add cream, season to taste, and bring just to boil. Transport in Ziploc freezer bag or plastic container, refrigerated or frozen.

To Pack: Hash, cream.

In Camp: Heat hash gently with extra cream, if necessary for consistency. Serves 4.

Natchitoches Meat Pies

Even if you're no pastry cook, these are kind of fun to make.

FILLING

2 tablespoons all-purpose flour
1 tablespoon shortening
1/2 pound ground chuck
1 pound hot sausage, finely
  chopped or ground

3 cups chopped onions
1 cup chopped green onion
3 tablespoons chopped parsley
1 teaspoon garlic powder
Salt and pepper to taste

PASTRY

4 cups sifted all-purpose flour
2 teaspoons baking powder
1 teaspoon salt

1/2 cup melted shortening
2 eggs
1/4 cup milk

At Home: Make a light brown roux with flour and shortening. Add meats, vegetables, and seasonings, and cook until vegetables are soft. Make pastry by sifting flour, baking powder, and salt together, then mixing in combined shortening, beaten eggs, and milk. Roll pastry as thin as you can (some of you are better at this than I am). Using the cover of a metal coffeepot or saucepan about 4 inches in diameter, cut out dough in circles, fill sparingly, about 1 tablespoon, with meat mixture, and fold dough over, dampening edges with water and crimping with a fork. Bake at 350 degrees until pies are golden brown. Transport in Ziploc freezer bags, refrigerated or frozen, and treat them gently. Makes about 32 pies.

To Pack: Meat pies, dark plastic bag or foil.

In Camp: Remove pies from ice chest an hour or so before serving and place in dark plastic bag in the sun to warm. Or wrap in foil and heat in steamer. Or eat them air temperature. These sound like trouble, but you can make lots and freeze them for home lunches or snacks.

Katy's Pralines

1 1/4 cups sugar
3/4 cup brown sugar
2/3 cup milk
2 tablespoons white Karo syrup

1/2 stick butter
1 teaspoon vanilla
2 cups pecan halves

At Home: Combine first five ingredients in saucepan and cook until mixture forms a soft ball in cold water, about 8-10 minutes. Do not overcook. Cool slightly, about 3 minutes, then add vanilla and beat till creamy. Stir in pecans and drop onto buttered surface. Let harden and transport in small tin or oatmeal box. About 12 medium pralines.

To Pack: Pralines.

In Camp: Serve just one apiece. Or try to.

Spiced Tea

A stimulating change for inveterate or even occasional tea drinkers.

Per cup:

1 teaspoon tea or 1 tea bag plus one extra for the pot	Pinch cinnamon or 1 cinnamon stick per pot
1 cup boiling water	Small piece orange peel
2 cloves	Small piece lemon peel

At Home: Combine spices and citrus peel in Ziploc bag.

To Pack: Thermos of tea or spices, tea, water, strainer.

At Home or In Camp: Bring water to boil with spices and citrus peel. Add tea and steep for 5 minutes. Strain and pour into thermos or serve immediately.

Almond Butter on Wheat Crackers

Almond butter, that most versatile of health food treats, is delicious on wholewheat crackers. Add some pepper jelly for emphasis. Almond butter makes great toast and the best "peanut butter and jelly" sandwiches going.

Portuguese Green Salad

If you lack almond butter (and I hope you don't), serve this salad first to keep dangerous appetites at bay.

1 head romaine	1 red onion, sliced thin in rings
1 bunch watercress	1/2 cup oil-packed black olives
2 ripe tomatos, sliced thin (if the tomatos don't smell and taste good, forget it)	

DRESSING

1/4 cup olive oil	Coarse salt
1/4 cup fresh lemon juice	Freshly-ground pepper

At Home: Mix olive oil, lemon juice, salt and pepper, and transport in jar. Wash and dry greens and store in Ziploc bags.

To Pack: Dressing, romaine, watercress, tomato, onion, olives.

In Camp: Arrange vegetables on a tray and drizzle with dressing. Serves 6-8.

Fall / Down From Cloud Crossing

Pack and Paddle Courtbouillon

Joan Williams, owner of Pack and Paddle of Lafayette, Louisiana, sent this recipe, whose original came from the Club de Pauvre Garcon, one of the first outdoor clubs in the state. She tells us that when the "poor boys" arrived at their campsite, this sauce was set to "taree" or simmer on an open fire while the men fished for bass, bream, or sac-au-lait. I hope you have a "poor boy"(or girl) of your own to bring back the fish.

1/2 cup oil
1/2 cup all-purpose flour
1 large onion, chopped
3 large cloves garlic, minced
1 teaspoon thyme
1 teaspoon marjoram
1 bay leaf
1 1/2 teaspoon salt
1 teaspoon pepper
1/2 teaspoon cayenne or to taste

1/4 teaspoon cloves
1 (1-pound) can tomatoes, chopped
1 1/2 cans water
2 1/2 pounds fish steaks (bass, bream, catfish, anything you can catch, or any ultra fresh fish you buy the day of the trip)

At Home: In an iron pot or large iron skillet, combine oil and flour and cook roux until medium brown. Add onion and garlic and cook until golden. Then add seasonings, tomatoes and juice, and water, and taree for 1 hour until sauce is thick and savory. Transport in plastic bags, frozen, if you like.

To Pack: Sauce, fish, rice.

In Camp: Heat sauce in pot or skillet just to boiling, add fish steaks, cover, and simmer for 20 minutes or until they are just done. Serve over Boiled Rice. Serves 6-8.

Fall / Down From Cloud Crossing

Hot French Bread with Lagniappe

We now confront one of the thorniest problems of camp cookery: how to get the bread *hot*. If you can't wrap it in foil and heat it in the steamer, here's a suggestion.

In Camp: After spreading the large loaf with margarine and the optional minced garlic, minced parsley, minced green onion tops, grated Parmesan or some other good-melting cheese, wrap it in two thicknesses of heavy foil and give it to someone else, preferably an engineer. Ask him or her to rig up something to heat the bread *hot* without burning. This usually works. Maybe some day I'll try another reflector oven. Or patent my battery-powered bread-heating sock.

To Pack: Bread, butter, garlic, parsley, onion tops, cheese, foil, an engineer.

Chocolate Ice Chest Pudding

This takes just a few minutes to whip up, but tastes like you toiled much longer. Double the recipe if you like, but you'll need to make the pudding in two blender batches.

6 ounces semi-sweet chocolate chips

2 ounces unsweetened chocolate, cut in pieces

1 cup light cream

4 tablespoons milk

4 egg yolks

Graham crackers or other flat plain cookies

Whipped cream

At Home: Put chocolate chips and pieces in blender. Heat cream and milk and pour over chocolate. With motor on high, blend until smooth. Add egg yolks, let run 30 seconds. Layer graham crackers and pudding in straight-sided plastic container, making at least two layers of each and preferably more. Keeps for several days refrigerated.

To Pack: Pudding, heavy cream, whisk, small bowl.

In Camp: Serve pudding cold topped with whipped cream. Makes 4-6 rich servings.

4

On the Shores of Lake Pontchartrain: A Family Campout

Fall gets hectic. The phone rings every half hour (and rarely brings offers of help, encouragement, or even money), ironing in the laundry basket grows a foot a day, and for all your incessant raking, the pecan leaves doggedly fall and just as doggedly must be raked. My solution? Go camping, of course. Get away without delay to a place that reminds you of other things worth doing. I know a place where things worth doing come with the territory, particularly if you show up on a bright gold October weekend.

Fronting the muddy blue waters of Lake Pontchartrain east of Mandeville, Louisiana, Fontainebleau State Park is 2,700 acres of playground and game preserve, room enough to spread out, unwind, and restore perspective, even if you bring the kids. Here for an hour or a whole day you can sit on the sand beneath rusty-needled cypress and simply watch the cloudbanks sweep across

Photo by Hulin Robert.

A canopied campsite on Lake Ponchartrain's North Shore.

the endless blue dome of the Lake; you can squish through marsh
or magnolia forest on miles of known or little-known trails; you
can swing under live oaks, slide with the kids; you can paddle
Cane Bayou lakeward for a picnic; but best of all, you can just
spend time with that guy (or gal) and those kids you've been
meaning to talk to for some time now.

For information on the park:

Fontainebleau State Park
P. O. Box 152
Mandeville, LA 70448
504/626-8052

Check with them for camping
reservations.

Louisiana Office of State Parks
P.O. Box 44426
Baton Rouge, LA 70804
504/342-8111

Serious hikers, obtain a U.S.
Geological Survey map,
Mandeville Quadrangle, at map
or camping stores.

MENUS

(* indicates recipes given)

Breakfast

Apple, Fig, and Orange Compote*
Scrambled Oysters* • Bakery Wholewheat Rolls
Queen Mary Tea • Milk for Kids

Lunch

Genoa Minestrone*
Comice Pears
Italian Biscotti Cookies
Coffee • Milk for Kids

Dinner

Beachcomber's Clam Broth*
Mandeville Mixed Grill*
Fresh Vegetable Relish* • Hot French Bread
Natural Flavor Soft Drinks for Kids
Marshmallows for Kids
Kahlua Coffee*
Wine: Go shopping for a very tasty, very inexpensive red table
wine like J.W. Morris California Red Private Reserve

Fall / Shores of Lake Pontchartrain

Apple, Fig, and Orange Compote

2 large oranges
1/2 cup water
1/2 cup brown sugar
1/8 teaspoon nutmeg
1 stick cinnamon

1/4 teaspoon allspice
6 ounces dried figs, quartered
4 Golden Delicious apples,
    cut in 1/2-inch pieces

At Home: Grate outer skin from 1/2 orange. Section oranges and set aside. Mix water, sugar, spices, and grated peel and boil gently for 5 minutes. Add figs and simmer 15 minutes or until almost tender. Add apples and simmer 15 more minutes or until tender, adding more liquid if necessary. Let cool and add orange sections. Can be made up to 24 hours ahead. Refrigerate in plastic container.

To Pack: Compote.

In Camp: Serve cool. Serves 6.

Scrambled Oysters

Most delicious; after the trip you may want to file this recipe away for the holidays.

12 small oysters, drained
1/2 stick butter
6 large fresh eggs,
    beaten slightly

2 tablespoons cream
2 tablespoons minced parsley
Salt and pepper

To Pack: Oysters, butter, eggs and cream in jar, parsley, salt and pepper.

In Camp: Gently saute oysters in butter for a minute or so. Add eggs and cream and scramble very slowly until just set. Sprinkle with parsley, salt, and pepper. If the kids prefer plain scrambled eggs, be glad and eat the extra oysters yourself. Serves 6.

Fall / Shores of Lake Pontchartrain

Genoa Minestrone

So thick the spoon stands alone; so savory, too much is not quite enough.

1 cup white beans
1/4 pound thick-sliced bacon, chopped
1/2 pound ham, cut up
1/2 pound Italian sausage
3 large cloves garlic, minced
1 large onion, chopped
2 stalks celery, chopped
Salt, pepper, pinch of allspice
2 quarts beef stock
1 cup Italian red wine

1 (16-ounce) can plum tomatoes, cut up
1 zucchini, diced
2 carrots, sliced
2 large potatoes, diced
2 cups shredded cabbage
1/2 cup macaroni or other pasta
1 teaspoon dried basil or 1 sprig fresh or 1 tablespoon Pesto Sauce
1 teaspoon garlic powder
Parmesan cheese

At Home: Soak beans overnight. In skillet, fry meats until lightly browned. Remove sausage and slice. Put drained meats in large pot with beans, garlic, onion, celery, salt, pepper, allspice, stock, wine, and tomatoes. Cook until beans are not quite tender. Add zucchini, carrots, and potatoes and cook until potatoes are nearly tender. Add cabbage, macaroni, basil and garlic powder and cook until all ingredients are tender, adding more liquid if necessary. Grate about 1/2 cup fresh Parmesan and transport in Ziploc bag. Cool soup and transport refrigerated or frozen in widemouth jars or Ziploc freezer bags.

To Pack: Soup, Parmesan, Sierra cup ladle.

In Camp: Heat soup and garnish each serving with fresh Parmesan. Serves 8-10.

Fall / Shores of Lake Pontchartrain

Beachcomber's Clam Broth

Serve cups of this soup while the coals are mobilizing for the barbeque.

4 teaspoons minced garlic
4 tablespoons minced green
  onion
10 tablespoons olive oil
1/2 pound mushrooms, sliced
1 1/2 cups drained canned
  clams

2 1/2 cups bottled clam juice
1 cup canned chicken broth
1/4 teaspoon oregano
1 bay leaf
3 tablespoons minced parsley

At Home: Cook garlic and green onion in olive oil until golden, add mushrooms and cook over high heat, stirring, for 2 minutes. Add clams, clam juice, broth, oregano, bay leaf, and parsley. Simmer soup for 15 minutes. Refrigerate in widemouth jars.

To Pack: Soup.

In Camp: Serve soup very hot in insulated cups. Serves 6.

Mandeville Mixed Grill

1 1/2 pounds cubed sirloin
2 pounds hot sausage, cut in
  3-inch pieces

6 chicken breasts, cut
  in half

MARINADE

1 1/2 cups olive oil
Salt and pepper
2 cloves garlic, slivered

2 tablespoons Worcestershire
  sauce

At Home: Place meat in separate Ziploc freezer bags with a portion of the marinade.

To Pack: Meats, French bread, butter, foil, grill or portable barbeque, charcoal, starter, tongs.

In Camp: Grill meats over charcoal or wood fire on grill until done to taste. Serve meats with hot buttered French bread and Fresh Vegetable Relish. Serves 6-8.

Fresh Vegetable Relish

8 green onions, finely chopped
1 medium bell pepper,
    finely chopped
Small bag radishes, chopped
2 (2-inch) jalapeno peppers,
    minced

Paprika, salt, and pepper to
    taste
Juice of 1 lemon
5 tasty tomatoes, chopped
    small and drained

At Home: Combine ingredients except tomatoes, and carry refrigerated to camp in widemouth jar. Makes about 5 cups.

To Pack: Relish, tomato.

In Camp: Add tomatoes to relish. This is great on red beans and rice or Beans with Chili and Chaurice.

Kahlua Coffee

Kahlua
Dark roast coffee

Whipping cream
Grated orange peel (optional)

To Pack: Above ingredients, whisk.

In Camp: Whip cream. Pour coffee, add a splash of Kahlua, and top with whipped cream and a sprinkle of orange peel.

5

Atchafalaya:
River Swamp Canoe Camping

"If you travel through the river swamps of Louisiana, you may very well grow uneasy as the sun is going down." Author John McPhee wasn't with us canoeing the Atchafalaya Swamp that freezing, stormy November day, but he had it right. To the hapless group who'd paddled ever deeper into watery wilderness seeking high ground to camp on, "uneasy" was a pretty good, if mild, word for the way we felt about the sun going down.

As it happened, we finally made landfall, though with barely light enough to figure the geometry of scrunching several hundred square feet of angular tents onto about the same square footage of shrinking mud bank just inches above the Atchafalaya Floodway.

Unbelievable as it seems, this was a trip people had actually paid to attend; consequently, I'd gone to special pains to bring along quantities of comforting food. Little did I realize how significant those meals were to become.

Only the temporary amnesia of our prolonged cocktail hour, followed by non-stop quarts of cassoulet managed to dull the lingering exhaustion of our icy paddle in the rain. With the demise of the rum cakes, we collapsed en masse and slept like the dead while the rising water lapped its way under our tents (actually floating us on our sleeping pads above the waterproof floors). Finally in the predawn hours, the tent floors gave way and let it *all* in, forcing most of us out under the tarp where we dozed fitfully and vertically til dawn. The only thing that revived our will to live, thereafter, was breakfast... that and three cups per of steaming hot coffee.

I don't know what this trip taught its other survivors—possibly never to paddle the river swamp with me or my partner—but what it taught me I've never forgotten: more than any other single factor, food is an achievable, predictable comfort to carry with you when camping. *Never* underestimate how much it matters.

Exploring the Atchafalaya Swamp is not supposed to be an ordeal. In spring and fall when water levels are high enough but not too high, it's a marvelous place to see wilderness and wildlife.

For information on the Atchafalaya:

Department of Transportation
and Development
Office of Public Works
P. O. Box 44155
Capitol Station
Baton Rouge, LA 70804

They'll tell you about the trip we took, Little Bayou Sorrel to Bayou Cocodrie to Flat Lake, and provide a map of the whole Atchafalaya Basin.

The sun sinks low in the Atchafalaya.

MENUS

(* indicates recipes given)

Breakfast

Tomato Juice and Lemon Wedges
Eggs Abbey* • Cajun Hash Browns*
Thick-Sliced Bacon
Creole Dripped Coffee*

Lunch

Uncle Spiffy's Barbequed Beef Buns*
Naval Oranges • Van Holten Garlic Pickles
Rich Camp Cocoa*

Dinner

Cheese Board*: Cheshire, Gruyere, Brie, Roquefort Cheese Ball
Wheat Crackers • Ripe Green and Black Olives
Atchafalaya Cassoulet* • Dark Rye Loaves
Swamp Salad with Louisiana Dressing*
Rum Cakes*
Wine: Reward yourself with a plummy red like
Robert Mondavi Pinot Noir

Eggs Abbey

The eggs honor the author of *Desert Solitaire*, Ed Abbey, a man
who knows all about living well in the wilderness.

1/2 cup chopped mild green chilis, fresh or canned	16 large eggs 2 tablespoons butter

At Home: To save ice chest space, crack eggs and transport in
plastic jar.

To Pack: Butter, eggs, chilis.

In Camp: Melt butter, add peppers and saute briefly; stir in eggs
and cook over low heat. Take your time. Serves 8-10.

Cajun Hash Browns

These spicy spuds will warm you up no matter where you are. Try some at Louie's Cafe in Baton Rouge where the insouciant fry cooks toss them two feet in the air and never miss a lick.

1/4 teaspoon garlic powder	1 small bell pepper, chopped
1/2 teaspoon pepper	1 tablespoon jalapeno pepper,
1 teaspoon salt	chopped
1/8 teaspoon cayenne	1 large onion, chopped
1/2 teaspoon paprika	3 large potatoes
1/4 teaspoon chili powder	1/2 stick margarine
1/4 teaspoon white pepper	

At Home: Mix spices in a Ziploc bag. Boil halved potatoes and transport in Ziploc bag.

To Pack: Spice bag, potato bag, peppers, onion, margarine.

In Camp: Chop peppers and onion. Melt margarine in non-stick skillet and saute peppers and onion for 3 minutes. Add diced potatoes and spices. Toss and stir for 5 minutes, then press down in pan with spatula and allow bottom to brown. Turn mixture over and brown other side. Serve at once. (To save a pan, fry bacon and set aside on paper towels. Use same pan to fry potatoes, omitting some of the margarine.) Makes 4 generous servings.

Creole Dripped Coffee

Here's a recipe for coffee in which the spoon practically stands alone.

To Pack: Coffee, drip coffee pot, water, sugar, cream.

In Camp: In a drip coffee pot place 2 heaping tablespoons dark roast grounds for every cup of coffee you want. Pour 2 tablespoons boiling water over grounds every 2-3 minutes until you have the right quantity. Sugar it up, cream it up and *savor*.

Fall / Atchafalaya

Uncle Spiffy's Barbequed Beef Buns

Most people can eat three of these, so be generous. Uncle Spiffy ate five studying for a dairy science final in 1961.

3 pounds boneless beef
  chuck roast
1/4 cup bacon drippings
1 large onion, chopped fine
2 large cloves garlic, crushed
1 cup catsup
2 tablespoons Worcestershire
1 tablespoon A-1 or
  Pickapeppa Sauce

3 dashes Tabasco or to taste
Smoke flavoring to taste
2 tablespoons chili powder
1 teaspoon ginger
2 tablespoons vinegar
Salt and pepper to taste
1/2 sliced lemon, seeded
2 cups water or more as needed

At Home: Slowly brown meat in bacon drippings in Dutch oven. Add remaining ingredients and cook, covered, very slowly for most of the day until the meat is fork tender. Add more liquid, if necessary. When meat is cool, slice and shred it into sauce. Refrigerate or freeze in Ziploc freezer bag or plastic container.

To Pack: Barbequed beef, buns.

In Camp: Heat meat and sauce and serve on hamburger rolls or buns. Serves 8.

Rich Camp Cocoa

1 tablespoon cocoa
  (Droste's is best)
1 tablespoon sugar or to taste

1/8 teaspoon vanilla
1/2 cup evaporated milk
1/2 cup water

At Home: Mix cocoa, sugar, and vanilla in plastic bag.

To Pack: Cocoa mixture, evaporated milk, water, whisk.

In Camp: Whisk cocoa mixture into milk and water and heat. Make this in the morning and carry in thermos for lunch. Makes 1 serving.

Cheese Board

Shop, if possible, in a real cheese store, ask for recommendations, and taste before you buy. Too often, I've brought home cheese from the supermarket tasting like disinfectant or worse.

Roquefort Cheese Ball

1/2 pound Roquefort
1/4 pound cream cheese
Juice of 1 small onion

Several shakes Tabasco
1 tablespoon Worcestershire
Minced pecans

At Home: Soften Roquefort and cream cheese and blend with mixer. Add onion juice, Tabasco, and Worcestershire. Roll into ball. Chill. Roll in minced pecans, wrap in foil, then in Ziploc bag and keep cold.

To Pack: Cheeses, crackers, cheese spreader.

In Camp: Serve cheese on crackers. Serves about 6-8.

Atchafalaya Cassoulet

This dish has turned around many a trip when the weather blew rainy or cold. Good insurance.

1 pound small white beans
Water to cover
1 bay leaf
1 teaspoon thyme
Freshly-ground pepper to taste
4 medium onions, chopped
1/2 pound veal, cubed
1/2 pound lean pork, cubed

4 ounces olive oil
1 cup dry white wine
1/2 pound miniature smoked
  pork sausages
1/4 pound ham, cut up
3 slices lean bacon, cut up
4 large garlic cloves, minced
Salt to taste

At Home: Soak beans overnight, rinse, cover with water, add bay leaf, thyme, pepper, and onions. Simmer, covered, 1 hour, adding more water if necessary. Saute veal and pork in olive oil till nearly tender. Add wine, and simmer 10 minutes. Saute sausage, ham, and bacon 5 minutes; drain and add to beans along with garlic. Add water for more liquid, if necessary and simmer till all ingredients are tender. Season with salt to taste. Cool and refrigerate or freeze in plastic container or Ziploc freezer bags.

To Pack: Cassoulet.

In Camp: Heat till bubbling hot (watch for scorching). Makes 4 generous servings and probably no more. Folks eat incredible quantities.

Swamp Salad with Louisiana Dressing

1 small green Creole cabbage, chopped
3 cups fresh kale leaves (you may have to grow this, but it's easy)
1 mild white onion, sliced thin
3 ribs bright green celery, diced

3 medium fresh carrots, sliced in thin coins
1/2 red pepper, diced small
1/2 yellow pepper, diced small
1/2 green pepper, diced small

LOUISIANA DRESSING

1/4 cup parsley, chopped
1/4 cup chives, chopped
1/4 cup celery, minced
2/3 cup olive oil

1/3 cup wine vinegar
1 teaspoon paprika
1 teaspoon salt
3 teaspoons Creole mustard

At Home: Wash vegetables, drain well, and carry to camp in plastic bags. Refrigerate. Mix dressing and carry in jar.

To Pack: Greens bag, veggie bag, jar of dressing, tongs.

In Camp: Prepare vegetables. Toss salad in giant bowl or pot, then add modest amount of dressing and toss again.

Rum Cakes

The canned rum cakes, 4 to a can by LaVille, are simple to serve and quite delicious. Heat the cans in simmering water prior to opening. If you really want to show off, top the cakes with whipped cream and garnish with sliced kiwi, strawberries or peaches.

To Pack: Rum cakes, cream, fruit, can opener, small bowl, whisk.

Fall / Atchafalaya

165

6

Thanksgiving in the Smokies:
Holiday Group Camping

The Great Smoky Mountains National Park, throbbing with motorists and crawling with summer campers, is a very different place from the one where we celebrated—*really* celebrated—our Thanksgiving holiday not long ago.

At Elkmont Campground, our four families were lucky enough to beat out the competition for four adjoining campsites insulated from other campers by strategic spruces and the soothing roar of a black and foaming mountain stream. From our base camp we set out on mountain trails still green with rhododendron, sharing child care and hot coffee, returning in time to collaborate on a

Crisp fall leaves blanket a Smoky Mountain clearing.

grand Thanksgiving dinner—a whole smoked turkey, marinated shrimp, spicy dressing, and pies—that wasn't so much excessive as it was just exactly right. The next morning, without warning, it was snowing; and for South Louisianians who see snow maybe once in ten years, it was icing on the cake.

For more information on Great Smoky Mountains camping:

Great Smoky Mountains
National Park
Gatlinburg, TN 37738
615/436-5615

The Park Service cuts back on camping space during Thanksgiving so be sure to check with them before you plan your trip.

MENUS
(* indicates recipes given)

Breakfast
Sausage in Onion Sauce*
Crunchy Wheat Bread*
Baked Green Apples with Cream*
Darjeeling Tea

Lunch
Chili Con Carne Muy Macho*
Waverly Wafers and Vermont Cheddar
Honey-Dipped Pineapple and Papaya
Coffee

Dinner
Seductresses' Shrimp Bowl*
Smoked Turkey* • Fresh Cranberry Relish*
Cornbread and Andouille Dressing*
Mashed Potatoes and Gravy
Hot Rolls and Butter
Cold Broccoli in Oil and Lemon*
Mrs. Tucker's Pecan Pie*
Wine: A delicious and complex red like Preston Zinfandel
Coffee

Sausage in Onion Sauce

Succulent sausage in a hearty peasant-style sauce makes great breakfast eating.

3 pounds fresh sausage (Spanish, Italian, or country-style)
3 cups thinly sliced onions
3 tablespoons butter
3 tablespoons all-purpose flour
2 teaspoons prepared mustard
3 cups beef broth
2 teaspoons sugar
1/2 teaspoon thyme
Salt and pepper to taste

At Home: Simmer pricked sausage in water to cover for 30 minutes. Cut sausage into 1/2-inch slices. Saute onions in butter until golden. Add flour and mustard and cook, stirring, for 3 minutes. Remove pan from heat and add beef broth, sugar, thyme, salt and pepper to taste. Bring to a boil and simmer, covered, for 1/2 hour. Add sausage and transport refrigerated or frozen in Ziploc freezer bags.

To Pack: Sausage.

In Camp: Simmer until sausages are heated through. Serves 6.

Crunchy Wheat Bread

The best wholewheat bread I've found.

1/2 cup wheat berries (from health food store)
1 tablespoon dry yeast
1/4 cup warm water
1 2/3 cups scalded and cooled milk
1/3 cup honey
2 tablespoons melted butter
2 teaspoons salt
5 1/2-6 1/2 cups whole wheat flour
1/2 cup wheat germ

At Home: Simmer wheat berries in water to cover until soft, about 3 hours. Dissolve yeast in warm water. Mix together milk, honey, melted butter, and salt. Stir in 4 cups flour and beat until dough is smooth. Then add remaining flour and wheat germ to make a stiff dough, using floured hands. Knead dough on floured board, adding more flour if necessary but keeping dough as soft as you can. When dough is smooth, put in greased bowl covered with a damp towel and let rise double. Punch down and knead in drained wheat berries. Divide dough in two loaves, place in greased pans, cover and let rise till almost double. Bake at 375 degrees about 45 minutes until browned. Wrap bread tightly in aluminum foil. Makes 2 loaves.

To Pack: Bread, butter.

In Camp: Serve warm with butter.

Fall / Thanksgiving in the Smokies

Baked Green Apples with Cream

Today's cooks often overlook this old-fashioned, but ever-tasty treat.

Medium-sized hard green apples (or Delicious or Rome Beauty)	Golden raisins
	Brown sugar
	Butter
Chopped walnuts	Water

At Home: Preheat oven to 350 degrees. Core apples to 1/2 inch of bottom and cut slices from top and bottom. Combine equal parts walnuts, raisins, and brown sugar and stuff apples. Top with pat of butter. Bake about 1/2 hour in baking dish in 1/2 inch hot water, until tender but not mushy. Wrap each apple in foil and transport in Ziploc freezer bag or plastic container.

To Pack: Apples, cream, steamer.

In Camp: Heat foil-wrapped apples in steamer and serve with cream.

Chili Con Carne Muy Macho

1 1/2 pounds coarse-ground beef	1 quart chopped fresh or canned tomatoes
1 pound coarse-ground or shredded pork	2 bay leaves
2 tablespoons chopped garlic	1 tablespoon oregano
1 large onion, chopped	1 tablespoon salt
1 tablespoon oil	4 teaspoons cumin
1/2 cup fresh chili pepper pulp, Anaheim or jalapeno (Okay, you can substitute canned, but it won't be the same dish.)	1 tablespoon garlic powder
	1 teaspoon pepper
	3 cups water, more if necessary
	2 (1-pound) cans red beans
	Sour cream, (optional)

At Home: Saute beef, pork, garlic, and onion in oil until meat is browned. Prepare chili pulp by searing peppers 2 inches under preheated broiler, turning every 5 minutes until chilis blister and char. Wearing rubber gloves if peppers are hot (and they ought to be), remove skin and seeds, and chop pulp. If you use canned peppers, chop them. Add chili, tomatoes, bay leaves, oregano, salt, cumin, garlic powder, pepper, and water and simmer 1 1/2 hours, adding more water if necessary. Refrigerate or freeze and transport in Ziploc freezer bags or widemouth plastic jars.

To Pack: Chili, 2 cans red beans, sour cream (optional).

In Camp: Heat chili and add 2 cans red beans. The steaming chili is good garnished with cold sour cream. Makes 10 servings.

Seductresses' Shrimp Bowl

Half the campers at Elkmont were hanging around our camp trying to seduce the cooks out of this recipe.

1 lemon, thinly sliced	1/2 bay leaf
1 onion, thinly sliced	1 tablespoon dry mustard
1/2 cup pitted ripe olives, sliced	1/4 teaspoon cayenne
1/2 cup lemon juice	1 tablespoon salt
1/4 cup olive oil	Freshly-ground black pepper to taste
1 tablespoon wine vinegar	2 pounds medium shrimp, boiled and peeled
1 clove garlic, minced	

At Home: Combine ingredients and refrigerate in plastic container or jar.

To Pack: Container of shrimp, wooden bowl, toothpicks.

In Camp: Serve day after preparing in wooden bowl with toothpicks for spearing. Serves 10.

Smoked Turkey

If you're into smoking turkeys, then by all means smoke your own. I'm not, so if we're camping with a large group, I buy a lightly-smoked, fully cooked, juicy hen turkey and bring the whole thing, resplendent in three layers of heavy aluminum foil in its own ice chest.

Heating it is a chore. Rule one: start early, at least two hours before dinner, preferably more. I hope you'll be situated at a campsite with a grill and picnic table for this production. If not, bring a folding table and a folding grill. Make a big fire and let it burn down to coals, then top with the grill. Wearing your barbeque mitts, place the turkey on the grill and turn it patiently, so that it heats gradually and evenly. The drama of a whole turkey served smoking hot is worth the effort, and of course you'll assign this job to someone else, rewarding him or her frequently with shrimp and wine.

Alternatively, you can roast a turkey at home, slice the meat and freeze it, reheating it efficiently and tamely in camp. Or you can have your butcher bone a turkey for you to roast at home and reheat it in a large double boiler in camp. Whatever your method, I predict Thanksgiving dinner outdoors will be your most memorable meal of the year.

Fresh Cranberry Relish

1 quart fresh cranberries, washed and picked over	1 large seedless orange
	1 cup sugar

At Home: Using a food grinder on coarse blade, or a food processor, or a sharp knife, reduce the whole orange and the cranberries to a finely-chopped hash. Stir in sugar and refrigerate in plastic container. This relish keeps well.
Makes 2 1/2 cups.

To Pack: Relish.

In Camp: Serve cold with hot turkey or to cheer up a leftover turkey sandwich.

Cornbread and Andouille Dressing

This dressing is good and spicy and doesn't lack flavor for baking outside rather than inside the turkey.

4 tablespoons margarine	2 pounds chicken or turkey
2 cups chopped celery	giblets (hearts, livers,
1 cup chopped green pepper	gizzards) boiled and
2 cups chopped onion	chopped (reserve broth)
1 cup chopped green onions	1/2 teaspoon black pepper
3/4 pound andouille sausage, chopped	1/2 teaspoon white pepper
	1/4 teaspoon cayenne
1 teaspoon minced garlic	2 teaspoons salt or to taste
1 (8-ounce) skillet Mexican	1/2 teaspoon thyme
cornbread from mix, crumbled	1/2 bunch parsley, cut fine
4 cups stale French bread, cubed	2 eggs, beaten

At Home: Saute celery, green pepper, onion, and green onion in margarine for 5 minutes. Add sausage and fry until vegetables are soft. Add garlic, cornbread, French bread, giblets, and seasonings and saute 10 minutes. Add broth and beaten eggs to mixture until it holds together without sogginess. Bake in greased baking dish for 30 minutes at 300 degrees. Cool thoroughly and refrigerate or freeze in Ziploc freezer bags.

To Pack: Dressing.

In Camp: Heat with small amount water. Serves 8-12.

Cold Broccoli in Oil and Lemon

1 bunch fresh broccoli
4 tablespoons olive oil
1/4 teaspoon oregano

1 clove garlic, minced
Salt
Freshly ground pepper

At Home: Trim the broccoli, slice each head lengthwise into quarters, and cook them tender-crisp in boiling water. Mix olive oil, oregano, garlic, salt and pepper, and pour over drained broccoli. Refrigerate in plastic bowl or container.

To Pack: Broccoli, 1 lemon.

In Camp: Squeeze half the lemon over the broccoli and decorate with slices of the other half. Serves 4-6.

Mrs. Tucker's Pecan Pie

This pie never fails to bring high praise, yet it's simple to make. Caution: Taste your pecans first to make sure they're fresh.

1 (10-inch) pie shell
1 cup sugar
2 tablespoons flour
2 eggs, lightly beaten

1 tablespoon butter
3/4 cup dark Karo syrup
1 teaspoon vanilla
1 cup whole pecans

At Home: Make or buy prepared pie shell. Mix ingredients in order in bowl and pour into unbaked shell. Bake at 350 degrees for 35-40 minutes or until filling no longer "moves." Do not overbake! Transport in cake tin cushioned with waxed paper.

To Pack: Pie.

In Camp: Warm pie by setting it near the fire and giving it a turn every now and then. Serves 6-8.

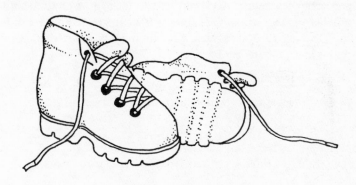

Fall / Thankgiving in the Smokies

Winter

Ribbons of ice glaze a Louisiana swamp.

1

Tangipahoa, The River We Call Home:
A Family Reunion Canoe Trip

To the five Wilcox kids growing up in Hammond, Louisiana, the Tangipahoa River, fishy and intriguing, was a place of mystery. We watched it flowing clear and bright in summer and fall, full and brown in spring and winter—always promising us more than the family picnics or high school beach parties we spread across its hospitably ample beaches. But not until we discovered canoeing did we really come to know the river we now call home.

Since then it has been a rare occasion when my far-flung brothers and sisters homing south for the winter don't volunteer for or get dragged on a Tangipahoa canoe trip, winter being the best time to be on the river. For one thing, no one else is. And even after 30 years the Tangi is still the same mysterious place it always was, springing surprise beaches on us or disguising our old campsites with upstart sycamore and river birch.

Meanwhile, every winter the Wilcox kids are out watching the old river roll, stopping to paint our faces with its rose-colored and gold clay, squelching through rustling reeds to inspect a beaver dam, still trying to catch its mean old catfish. I don't see an end to any of it soon.

For information on the Tangipahoa River:

Riverside Canoe Rentals
Rt.2, Box 1-C
Amite, LA 70422
504/748-4878

Canoe and tube rental, shuttles, river information.

MENUS

(*indicates recipes given)

Breakfast

Cajun Cocktail*
Scrambled Egg Pie*
Cheese Danish Pastries*
Homemade Coffee*

Lunch

Creole Vegetable Soup*
Saga Cheese on Party Rye
Homemade Coffee
Pepperidge Farm Florentine Cookies

Dinner

Jack Daniels on the Rocks* • Barbecued Pecans
Tony's Creole Stuffed Pork Roast*
Dirty Rice* • J.D.'s Yams*
Satsumas and Bittersweet Chocolate*

Cajun Cocktail

This actually improves with age and would be delicious for a summer lunch, although I suppose you'd need a fresh batch.

4 cups tomato juice
1 medium cucumber, peeled
   and finely chopped
2 tablespoons minced
   green onion
Juice of 1 lemon

1 tablespoon Worcestershire
1/2 teaspoon grated lemon rind
2 teaspoons horseradish
1 clove garlic, peeled
   and crushed
4 shakes Tabasco or more

At Home: In glass juice container combine ingredients, mix, and refrigerate.

To Pack: Cajun Cocktail.

In Camp: Serve cold while the Scrambled Egg Pie cooks. Serves 6-8.

Scrambled Egg Pie

Because potatoes hold the heat well, this is an excellent cold-weather breakfast. The only drawback—for best results you need to haul an iron skillet.

Leftover mashed potatoes	Milk
Salt, pepper, cayenne	Eggs
Butter	Bacon

At Home: Season mashed potatoes with salt, pepper, and cayenne, and transport in plastic bag. If ice chest space is tight, crack eggs into plastic jar for transport. Cook bacon crisp and crumble into plastic bag.

To Pack: Mashed potatoes, eggs, bacon, milk, butter, optional garnishes, 8-inch iron skillet.

In Camp: Add extra milk and butter to potatoes in plastic bag to make them pliable. In iron skillet, melt generous quantity of butter and add potatoes, pressing down with spoon to form a bowl shape. While potatoes heat, scramble eggs in another skillet, adding crumbled bacon halfway through cooking. When eggs are done and potatoes very hot and slightly browned on bottom, fill potato shell with scrambled eggs and bacon and serve at once. Variation: Other ingredients such as chopped green onion on top of eggs, chilis in them, or cheese under them are good. This is also extra fine filled with Scrambled Oysters. An 8-inch skillet serves about 4.

Cheese Danish Pastries

Buy these at the bakery on the way out of town and heat in foil or steam slightly to restore freshness.

Homemade Coffee

As every camper knows, the low spot on a camping trip is often the pre-breakfast funk that sets in if the night's mood was festive and no one picked up the wine bottles or washed the spaghetti pot. A good antidote is fresh hot coffee ready *immediately*. Bring it already made extra-strong from home, transported in a sturdy glass juice container, and kept cold until you pour it into the bottom of a drip pot. Don't underestimate coffee's allure as a bribe for reluctant pot-washers.

Creole Vegetable Soup

This makes tons, but it's handy to have extra in the freezer for Sunday night suppers.

2 pounds beef shank	3 quarts water
1 large onion, chopped	2 ribs celery, chopped
2 ribs celery, chopped	2 large potatoes, diced
1 teaspoon pepper	1 large tomato, cut up
1/4 teaspoon cayenne	1 cup frozen lima beans
1/4 teaspoon chili powder	3 carrots, chopped
2 teaspoons salt	1 cup frozen corn
1 teaspoon garlic powder	1 onion, chopped

Other vegetables: fresh string beans, frozen peas, turnips, cabbage—about a cup of any or all.

At Home: Simmer meat in seasoned water with 1 chopped onion and 2 ribs chopped celery until meat is nearly tender, about 2 hours. Add remaining ingredients and simmer until all are tender. If you use cabbage, add it toward latter part of cooking. Correct seasoning, cool soup, freeze, if desired, and carry to camp in widemouth plastic jar or plastic pitcher. Makes about 16 cups.

To Pack: Soup, Sierra cup ladle.

In Camp: Heat gently and serve in insulated cups.

Jack Daniels on the Rocks

You've got to be careful with this recipe—a little goes a long way. Still, there are some fine and festive occasions, particularly cold-weather trips, when nothing warms like a little high-priced bourbon.

Tony's Creole Stuffed Pork Roast

A delicious and deadly dish, best eaten beside a wind-whipped campfire.

5 pounds pork loin or rolled pork roast	1/2 green pepper, finely chopped
2 tablespoons Tony's Creole Seasoning (chili powder, garlic powder, paprika, cayenne, salt, and pepper)	1 large clove garlic, minced
	2 stalks celery, finely chopped
	2 tablespoons oil
1 large onion, finely chopped	2 cups water

At Home: Rub meat with 1 tablespoon seasoning. Mix 1 table-spoon seasoning with chopped vegetables. Cut about 10 slits in meat and stuff each with seasoned vegetable mix. Brown roast in oil in Dutch oven, adding remaining vegetables during latter part of browning. Add 2 cups water and cover meat, allowing it to braise for 2 or 3 hours until meltingly tender. Add more water, if necessary. Cool and transport to camp in Ziploc freezer bags.

To Pack: Pork roast.

In Camp: Heat meat gently, adding more water for a thin ambrosial gravy. Serves about 10.

Dirty Rice

1 pound chicken giblets
including livers
Salt, pepper, cayenne
to taste (use a lot)
1 quart water
1/3 cup oil
3 tablespoons all-purpose
flour

1 pound ground pork or beef
2 cups chopped onion
2 cups chopped celery
6 cups cooked rice
(about 2 cups raw)
1/2 cup chopped green
onion tops
1/4 cup chopped parsley

At Home: Season giblets with salt, pepper, and cayenne and boil in water until tender. Remove, reserving broth, and chop fine. Make a roux of the oil and flour and cook, stirring constantly, until medium brown. Add the ground meat and the onion and celery and cook until meat is browned and onion clear. Add chopped giblets, stock, more seasoning, and cook 10 minutes or until meats and vegetables are tender and flavors blended. Stir in cooked rice and mix well over low heat. Stir in green onion tops and parsley. Cool quickly, preferably spread out in baking pan. then pack into Ziploc freezer bags and freeze if you like. This dish must be handled carefully, kept very hot or very cold as the chicken livers are perishable. If you follow directions, don't worry.

To Pack: Dirty Rice.

In Camp: Heat with a very little water and fluff with fork. Serves 8-10.

J.D.'s Yams

7 medium yams,* peeled
   and sliced 1-inch thick
1 cup brown sugar
1/4 teaspoon cinnamon

Water just to cover yams
1/2 stick margarine or butter
A splash of Jack Daniels
   bourbon

At Home: Boil yams in brown sugar, water, and cinnamon until tender but not mushy. If yams get tender before water cooks down to syrup, remove them and continue cooking liquid until syrupy. Place yams, syrup, and butter in pieces in Ziploc freezer bag and transport to camp.

  *What we call yams are really sweet potatoes.

To Pack: Yams, bourbon.

In Camp: Heat yams in syrup to which you have added a splash of JD for interest. Serves 10.

Satsumas and Bittersweet Chocolate

If anyone is fool enough to want dessert after such a meal, all I can suggest is the clean tart refreshment of a satsuma or tangerine and a small bite of bittersweet Lindt Swiss chocolate which is even better heated on a skewer over the fire. According to M.F.K. Fisher, the slyest, suavest gastronome alive, when the chocolate gives off a "dark blue smell" (almost burnt), it is ready.

Venturing out to discover the secrets of the Tangi.

2

Kisatchie Bayou A Deux:
A Couple's Weekend Getaway

For all our laudable efforts to be good parents, good sons and daughters, good workers, good friends,and good citizens, many couples, myself and my husband included, sometimes forget the importance of being good to one another. When this happens, we know it's time for a camping trip *a deux.*

On these private occasions, a place we've returned to again and again is Kisatchie Bayou Camp, whose primitive walk-in sites to

Good talk comes easy on a camping trip for two.

a stream in the Kisatchie National Forest near Alexandria, Louisiana, are as free from distraction as any I know. On a recent trip shortly after Christmas which had closely followed a warm fall, the woods bordering the inky bayou were blazing with crimson swamp maples and buttergold beeches. It wasn't terribly Christmassy—more like New Hampshire in early fall, but what a splendid place to walk, talk, and laugh together. And the food, so simple and so good, made it even better.

For information on camping in the Kisatchie National Forest:

Supervisor's Office
Kisatchie National Forest
2500 Shreveport Highway
Pineville, LA 71360
318/473-7123

MENUS
(*indicates recipes given)

Breakfast
Poached Eggs in Cream*
Holland Rusks
Cherry Preserves
Indian Spiced Tea Balaji*

Lunch
Hot Sausage on Rye*
Carrot Sticks
Ginger Cookies*
Coffee

Dinner
Mixed Nuts
Platonic Shrimp Fettuccini*
Green Beans Au Natural*
Frostproof Peach Pudding*
Wine: If you can afford it, a soul-tingling white
like de Ladoucette Pouilly-Fumé

Poached Eggs in Cream

1 tablespoon butter
4 thin slices ham
1/2 cup light cream

1/2 teaspoon curry powder
4 jumbo eggs
Salt and pepper to taste

At Home: Combine cream and curry powder in jar.

To Pack: Butter, ham, cream and curry mix, eggs, salt, pepper, and Holland rusks.

In Camp: Fry ham in butter in small nonstick skillet until hot and browned. Place ham on Holland rusk, wrap in foil, and set on back of campstove or over tea water to keep warm. In same skillet, bring cream to boil and simmer 30 seconds before carefully adding eggs. Poach by spooning cream over eggs until they are set. Salt and pepper eggs and serve on Holland rusk. Serves 2.

Indian Spiced Tea Balaji

2 cups water
2 teaspoons black tea
2 tea bags
1 1/2 inches stick cinnamon

4 whole cloves
1/8 teaspoon cardamom
1/2 cup milk
Brown sugar or honey

To Pack: Tea, spices, water, milk, brown sugar or honey, strainer.

In Camp: Place tea bags and spices in water and bring to boil. Boil 1 minute, then add milk and brown sugar or honey to taste. This interesting tea goes down easily; you may want to double the recipe for two.

Hot Sausage on Rye

If you'll eat lunch in camp, cook your sausage there. If you'll eat lunch on a hike, cook sausage after breakfast and wrap the sandwiches in foil.

Hot link sausage
Rye bread

Butter
Hot mustard

At Home or In Camp: Prick sausage with fork and cook in water to cover for 20 minutes. Drain and transport in Ziploc freezer bag.

To Pack: Sausage, rye bread, butter, mustard.

In Camp: Spread single slices of rye bread with butter and mustard and roll each slice around a sausage, heated or not.

Winter / Kisatchie Bayou A Deux

Ginger Cookies

These are wonderful for Christmas giving as well as for camping trips.

4 sticks butter or margarine	8 cups all-purpose flour
3 cups sugar	1 1/2 tablespoons each
1 cup molasses	baking soda and ginger
3 eggs	1 tablespoon cloves
1 teaspoon salt	1 tablespoon cinnamon

At Home: Cream butter, add sugar and beat till light. Add molasses and eggs, beating after each, and then add salt. In large bowl sift flour, baking soda, and spices. Stir flour mixture into butter. With sugar-coated hands, roll into 1 1/2-inch balls, roll balls in sugar and bake on ungreased sheet 2 inches apart for 12 minutes or until lightly browned. Transport in tin or oatmeal box. Makes about 70 cookies.

To Pack: Cookies, coffee, milk.

In Camp: Serve with coffee and milk.

Platonic Shrimp Fettuccini

Never knew haute New Orleans cuisine could go camping, did you?

1 pound medium shrimp	1/2 pound mushrooms
peeled and pristinely fresh	2 green onions
1 1/2 teaspoons salt	4 tablespoons parsley
1/4 teaspoon cayenne	8 ounces dried high-quality
1/2 teaspoon pepper	fettuccini (De Cecco,
1/2 teaspoon basil	for example)
1/2 teaspoon thyme	Salt
1/4 teaspoon oregano	1 stick butter
2 garlic cloves	

At Home: Peel shrimp and store in Ziploc freezer bag. (Where seafood is concerned, I use two to avoid the dread possibility of ice chest odor). In another Ziploc bag combine dry seasonings and 2 unpeeled garlic cloves. In third Ziploc bag combine washed mushrooms, green onions, and parsley.

To Pack: Shrimp bag, seasoning bag, veggie bag, fettuccini, salt, butter, water for pasta, steamer, skillet.

In Camp: Cook fettuccini al dente in boiling, salted water in bottom of steamer. Drain, toss with 1 tablespoon butter. Cover and keep warm. Slice mushrooms, chop green onions, and mince parsley. In skillet melt remaining butter over high heat. Add mushrooms, green onions, and seasonings, and cook for about 5 minutes, stirring. Add shrimp and cook for 5 minutes more. Add drained fettuccini and toss. Sprinkle with fresh parsley. Makes 2 generous servings.

Green Beans Au Natural

1/2 pound fresh green beans, trimmed   2 tablespoons butter
Salt and pepper

At Home: Boil beans in ample salted water to cover until bright green and barely tender. Drain and rinse with ice water. Transport in Ziploc bag.

To Pack: Beans, butter, salt and pepper.

In Camp: Heat beans in skillet with butter, salt and pepper. Transfer to foil package and keep warm over steamer while you prepare fettuccini in bottom. Makes 2 servings.

Frostproof Peach Pudding

Here's a dessert for arctic nights by the fire.

Pound cake (your own or Sara Lee)   Bourbon or brandy or heavy cream
Frozen peaches and juice

To Pack: Pound cake, peaches, bourbon, brandy, or cream.

In Camp: Break pieces of pound cake into an insulated cup. Add heated peaches and a shot of bourbon, brandy, or cream. Stir briskly and eat the same way. Variations: Substitute frozen dark sweet cherries for peaches.

Winter / Kisatchie Bayou A Deux

3

New Year's at Gulf State Park: A Winter Holiday in Alabama

New Year's is the time we resolve to trim down, smarten up, and fly right—just the right time to trade passive TV-watching for an active and unconventional beginning to a new year: a camping trip to Gulf Shores, Alabama.

You may be surprised to find that others have had the same idea, most of them "snowbirds" from the north who flock to the 468 campsites of huge, marvelous Gulf State Park. Alabama, let it be said, does not stint when it comes to its state parks—the ones I've seen are top-notch. Gulf State Park has everything you'll need for a winter holiday and more: miles of quiet roads for biking, a freshwater lake and Gulf fishing pier, unpolluted beaches, pine-shaded campsites, and a winter climate that ranges from

A sunset stroll along a deserted beach.

mild to biting, with warm spells interspersed. If you happen to hit the park at an intemperate moment, refuge is near in the form of 21 fully-equipped lakeside cottages or 144 beachside motel rooms, all part of the park. On our last trip to Gulf Shores, a rainy cold front blew us out of the campground and into the resort, not the worst ending for a winter holiday, believe me.

For information on Gulf State Park:

Gulf State Park
Route 2, Box 9
Gulf Shores, Al 36542
Toll-free 1-800-ALABAMA
Office and Cabin information: 205/968-7544
Campground: 205/968-6353 (Reservations are suggested.)
Resort Inn: 205/968-7531

Menus

(*indicates recipes given)

Breakfast

Grillades and Grits*
Banana Muffins*
Fresh Pears
Coffee

Lunch

Smoky Turkey and Sausage Gumbo*
Fresh Apple Cake*
Black Tea

3:00 Coffee Break

Hot Coffee
Italian Biscotti

Dinner

Green and Black Olives and Pickled Peppers*
Pork Chops in White Wine*
Spinach Fettuccini Bolognese*
Roman Ricotta Pie*
Wine: A crisp Italian, like Soave Bolla

Grillades and Grits

A rich and flavorful Creole breakfast dish, heartening to campers on a frosty morning.

4 pounds beef round or
　sirloin tip cut in 1/2-inch
　serving pieces
1/2 cup bacon drippings
1/2 cup all-purpose flour
1 cup chopped onion
1 cup chopped green
　pepper
1 stalk chopped celery
2 cloves garlic, minced

2 cups chopped tomato or
　1 (1-pound) can
1/2 teaspoon thyme
2 teaspoons salt
1/2 teaspoon black pepper
1/4 teaspoon cayenne
2 bay leaves
2 tablespoons Worcestershire
3 tablespoons parsley,
2 cups water

At Home: Brown meat in 1/2 the bacon grease and remove. Add remaining grease and flour, and cook to a dark roux. Add vegetables and cook until they are limp. Add tomatoes and seasonings and cook 3 minutes. Add water and meat and simmer, covered, until meat is fork tender. Transport meat and sauce in Ziploc freezer bag.

To Pack: Grillades, grits, salt.

In Camp: Serve with Go-For-It Grits. Serves 8-10.

Banana Muffins

Ultra-ripe bananas make a big difference in flavor.

2 cups (3 large) mashed
　overripe bananas
1 cup sugar
2 eggs
1 1/2 sticks margarine, melted
2 cups all-purpose flour

2 teaspoons baking soda
3 tablespoons buttermilk
　(make it with milk and a
　little vinegar or use powder-
　ed buttermilk and water)
1 cup chopped pecans

At Home: Combine banana, sugar, and eggs. Add margarine, mixing well. Stir in flour and baking soda, then add buttermilk and pecans. Spoon batter into 12 greased muffin cups and bake at 300 degrees until dark brown, about 1 hour. Let set 5 minutes and remove from pan. Transport in cake tin. Makes 1 dozen.

To Pack: Muffins, butter.

In Camp: Serve warm with butter.

Smoky Turkey and Sausage Gumbo

Freeze the remainder for a busy day supper.

1 turkey carcass	1 teaspoon thyme
Water to cover	1/2 teaspoon liquid smoke
1/2 cup flour	seasoning
1/2 cup oil	Salt, pepper, and cayenne
1 cup chopped green onion	to taste
2 cups chopped yellow onion	1 pound andouille or other
1 cup chopped green pepper	smoked sausage, cut up
1 cup chopped celery	1 pint oysters and liquor,
1/2 cup chopped parsley	(optional)
3 bay leaves	File powder

At Home: Bring turkey to boil in water to cover, then simmer until meat is tender. Remove meat and cook stock down to 3 quarts. Make a roux with the flour and oil and cook till dark brown. Add chopped green onion, yellow onion, green pepper, and celery to roux and cook, stirring, till vegetables are limp. Remove meat from carcass and chop into bite-size pieces.

Boil andouille briefly in water to cover. Rinse and drain. Add turkey, vegetables and roux, sausage, and seasonings except filé powder to broth and simmer 1 hour. Add oysters during last 5 minutes. Transport refrigerated or frozen in Ziploc freezer bags or plastic pitcher.

To Pack: Gumbo, rice, filé, Sierra cup ladle.

In Camp: Heat gumbo steaming hot, stir in a few tablespoons of file powder, and serve over cooked rice in insulated cups. Makes about 20 cups.

Winter / New Year's at Gulf State Park

Fresh Apple Cake

A down-home favorite and a real good keeper.

3 cups raw chopped,
peeled apples
2 cups sugar
1 1/2 cups oil
2 eggs, well-beaten
1 teaspoon salt

1 teaspoon cinnamon
1 teaspoon baking soda
3 cups all-purpose flour
1 teaspoon vanilla
3/4 cup broken pecans

At Home: Mix apple, sugar, oil, and eggs. Sift together salt, cinnamon, baking soda, and flour. Add sifted ingredients to apple mixture, then add vanilla and pecans. Bake at 350 degrees in 9x12x2-inch greased pan 50-60 minutes or till it tests done. Let cool, cut into squares, and transport in cake tin.

To Pack: Cake.

In Camp: Serve for lunch or next morning for breakfast. Makes 12-15 servings.

Green and Black Olives
and Pickled Peppers

Take the trouble to find the genuine article: imported Italian all the way. If you add Peppers Provencal, fried Italian sausage, and Italian bread, you've got a memorable lunch.

Pork Chops in White Wine

Another easy entree with a sophisticated taste.

1 teaspoon sage
1/4 teaspoon rosemary
1 teaspoon minced garlic
1 teaspoon salt
Freshly-ground pepper
4 center-cut pork chops,
   about 3/4-inch thick

1 tablespoon butter
1 tablespoon olive oil
1 cup white wine
1 tablespoon finely-chopped,
   parsley

At Home: Combine sage, crushed rosemary, garlic, salt, and freshly-ground pepper and rub onto pork chops. Melt butter with olive oil and brown chops, then remove from pan. Add 1/2 cup of the wine and bring to boil. Return chops to pan, cover, and simmer until tender, adding more liquid if necessary. Place chops in shallow plastic container, pour sauce over and sprinkle parsley over chops. Freeze, if desired.

To Pack: Pork chops, extra wine.

In Camp: Heat chops in sauce, adding more wine if necessary. Serves 4.

Spinach Fettuccini Bolognese

I guarantee this recipe will become a favorite. Try it.

1 (16-ounce) package spinach fettuccini, De Cecco or other high-quality brand
1 1/2 pounds ground chuck or round
2 slices lean salt pork or 6 slices bacon, finely chopped
1 large onion, finely chopped
1 carrot, finely chopped
1 stalk celery, finely chopped

2 cloves garlic, minced
1/4 cup parsley, chopped
4 tablespoons butter
1/2 cup stock or bouillon
1 tablespoon tomato paste or puree
Salt, pepper, and a pinch of nutmeg
1 cup heavy cream
1/4 cup freshly-grated Parmesan

At Home: Combine meats and vegetables and saute in butter until meat is browned. Add stock, tomato paste or puree, and seasonings to taste. Cook gently for 45 minutes, covered, adding more stock if necessary. During last 10 minutes of cooking, add cream and taste for seasoning. Cook fettuccini in boiling salted water al dente. Mix drained pasta with sauce and stir in Parmesan. Transport in Ziploc freezer bag. You can freeze this, but you will lose some texture in the process.

To Pack: Spinach Fettuccini Bolognese or sauce, pasta, salt, pot drainer, and water.

In Camp: Re-heat gently. For the best texture of all, cook fettuccini in camp and assemble dish there. Serves 4.

Roman Ricotta Pie

This recipe has been evolving for 2,000 years or more. Somewhere along the centuries it began to taste pretty good.

CRUST

2 cups all-purpose flour
1 1/2 sticks butter
4 egg yolks

1/4 cup sugar
1 teaspoon grated lemon peel

FILLING

5 cups ricotta cheese
  (2 1/2 pounds)
1/2 cup sugar
1 tablespoon flour
1 teaspoon vanilla

1 teaspoon grated orange peel
4 egg yolks
1 tablespoon golden raisins
2 tablespoons slivered almonds
Green grapes for garnish

At Home: Blend flour, butter, egg yolks, sugar, and lemon peel with a mixer or your fingertips. Gather dough together and work it with the heel of your hand until it forms a smooth ball. Chill.

Preheat oven to 350 degrees. Roll out 2/3 of dough until it is a thin circle. Place in 9-inch buttered tart or cakepan.

Combine ricotta with sugar, flour, vanilla, orange peel, egg yolks, and raisins. Partially bake pie crust until it begins to look hardened. Cool. Roll out remaining third of dough, cut in 1/2-inch strips. Spoon filling into pastry shell. Top with a lattice crust sprinkled with almonds. Bake pie for 1 hour or until crust is golden and filling firm. Cover with foil if crust browns too much. Chill, wrap in foil, and transport in its own pan, in cake tin padded with paper towels. Keep refrigerated.

To Pack: Pie, grapes.

In Camp: Serve in small wedges garnished with green grapes. Serves 8.

Winter / New Year's at Gulf State Park

4

The Swamp in Our Backyard:
A Moonlight Canoe Paddle

After three weeks of February rain, the Louisiana swamp is warming up, revving into the great green swell of spring. The black, gar-smelling water into which we launch this late Saturday afternoon is stirred by our canoe paddles into delicious-looking duckweed soup. We glide along Alligator Bayou under willows clink-

The pale moon silhouettes a moss-laden cypress.

ing with myrtle warblers, brimming with robins; above their gold-green light, the sky is enameled blue.

Alligator Bayou, Cypress Flats, and Spanish Lake—the waters that we ply are provinces of an Iberville Parish swamp so close to Baton Rouge that it feels like home to us River Rats. It's home, too, for red-tailed hawks and crows, for whooping barred owls, and for way too many nutria who this day have appropriated virtually every other emergent log for communal sunbathing.

The sun is sinking west, accelerating as it plunges home in a blaze of flamingo fire. We wait in our silent canoes for the return of the egrets and hope some of the fancier swamp folk, ibis perhaps, will accompany them to night-time roosts in the blackening cypress of the Flats.

Soon the moon will glaze the black water with light, the sight we've come to see, so we hunker down in our cold canoes with our hot food and spunky drinks, here to stay a while.

For information on Alligator Bayou:

Alligator Bayou Bait Shop
Bayou Billy, Manager
Rt. 2 Box 254
Iberville, LA 70746
504/642-8297

Canoe and bateau rental, live bait, coon meat and fish for sale.

Directions to Alligator Bayou: From I-10 or Airline Highway in Baton Rouge, take Perkins Road to Highway 928 (at Spanish Mansion). Go over I-10 and take first right at bottom of bridge (Alligator Bayou Road). Go 1 mile to Bait Shop which has a launch and rents canoes reasonably. Don't miss the Alligator Bar across the bayou, as welcoming in its offbeat way as the swamp itself.

MENU
(*indicates recipes given)

Sundown Supper

Hot Prince of Wales Tea or Spunk Juice* • Macadamia Nuts
Garlicky Onion Soup*
Hot Cuban Sandwiches*
Margie Galloway's Pineapple Pie*
Moonshine Coffee*

Spunk Juice

As good as hot tea for warding off a chill.

2 tablespoons Jack Daniels
  Black Label or other good
  bourbon
1 teaspoon honey

Juice of 1/2 lemon
Hot water to fill cup
Nutmeg

At Home: Mix ingredients in thermos for swamp paddlers in need of spunk.

To Pack: Thermos of Spunk Juice.

In Camp: Sip slowly from insulated cups as you watch the sun go down. Makes 1 cup.

Garlicky Onion Soup

This soup takes up warming where the Spunk Juice or tea left off.

4 medium onions, thinly
  sliced
3 tablespoons oil
8 cups beef stock
  (canned or homemade)

Salt and freshly-ground pepper
Pinch thyme
1 bay leaf
1 celery stalk, cut in pieces
6 whole peeled garlic cloves

At Home: Saute onion in oil until golden brown. Pour in stock, and seasoning and simmer, covered, for 10 minutes. Remove garlic and celery and pour into thermos jug.

To Pack: Onion soup, styrofoam cups.

In Camp: Serve in disposable styrofoam cups. To clean thermos after soup, first wash in suds and household ammonia, rinse thoroughly, then soak several hours in bleach solution, and again rinse thoroughly. The soup serves 6.

Winter / The Swamp in Our Back Yard

Hot Cuban Sandwiches

Do you think the Cubans under Castro still eat these decadent sandwiches? We can only hope.

Cuban or French bread loaves, about 6 inches long, split and buttered
Sliced Cuban Pork Roast
Sliced baked ham

Sliced Provolone, Jack, or other soft white cheese
Sweet pickle relish or Frozen Sweet Pickles

At Home: Layer ingredients on bread. Wrap sandwiches in foil and heat. Transport in small ice chest packed with napkins, newspaper, or paper towels to retain heat.

To Pack: Sandwiches.

In Camp: Serve at least one per person.

Cuban Pork Roast

4-5 pound pork roast
1 tablespoon chopped pickled jalapeno peppers
2 cloves garlic, minced

1/2 cup olive oil
1/4 cup cider vinegar
Freshly-ground pepper to taste

At Home: Marinate roast for 2 days in refrigerator in combined marinade ingredients. Turn roast occasionally and rub with marinade. Roast it at 300 degrees for 35-40 minutes per pound until meat thermometer inserted in thickest part is 165-170 degrees and meat is brown and tender.

Margie Galloway's Pineapple Pie

A rich, buttery pie, perfect for winter warm-ups.

CRUST

2 cups all-purpose flour
1 stick butter (no substitute)
3 tablespoons shortening

1/2 teaspoon sugar
Pinch salt
5-6 tablespoons ice water

FILLING

1 cup sugar
2 teaspoons all-purpose flour
3 eggs

1 stick melted butter
1 cup crushed pineapple (1 [20 ounce] can, well-drained)

At Home: For the shell: With electric mixer, blend flour, butter, shortening, sugar, and salt until mixture is uniformly crumbly. Add ice water and blend until dough holds together. Divide dough into two unequal size balls, wrap in plastic wrap and chill 1 hour. Roll out larger ball, fit into a 9-inch pie pan, and set aside. For the filling: Combine sugar and flour until well mixed; stir in eggs, melted butter, and very well drained pineapple (press juice out through a strainer).

Roll out remaining dough, cut in strips and arrange over filling in lattice pattern. Bake pie at 350 degrees until filling is firm and crust is golden, about 50 minutes. Wrap pie in foil and transport in warm insulated ice chest with sandwiches. Note: You'll probably have extra pastry left: roll it out, sprinkle it with sugar and cinnamon, bake till golden, and eat at once. The kids will love it and so will you.

To Pack: Pie, small paper plates.

In Camp: Serve pie warm, if it still is.

Moonshine Coffee

Gilding the lily? Perhaps. Still, if the night is cold and the moon slow to rise, give it a go. Simply add a splash of rum and a nip of honey to hot coffee in a thermos. (The point of all this heartening food and drink is to brace you to stay on in a place where most city folk either don't go or leave too soon.)

Winter / The Swamp in Our Back Yard

5

Mardi Gras in Mississippi:
An Opulent River Holiday

Most South Louisianians wouldn't miss Mardi Gras for money, and neither would we. The only difference is that, unlike the wall-to-wall revelers who fill Bourbon Street with their spilled beer, raucous chatter, and ape costumes, we break out the down jackets and the wool pants and take our wildness north of New Orleans to the Bogue Chitto River west of Tylertown, Mississippi.

Courtesy U.S. Forest Service (Mississippi

Moving the party downstream.

It's quieter there, crowds are thinner, and the river runs swift and silent past sandbars and claybanks and grey woods spattered with yellow jessamine.

But don't be fooled. Mardi Gras in the wilds of Mississippi is still Mardi Gras, the last big obligation to celebrate before a Lenten curtain falls on the prolonged holiday season. So party we do, just as intensely as anything going down in the Vieux Carre. We just like to think we do it with a little more taste.

Too bad not everyone agrees.

MENUS
(*indicates recipes given)

Breakfast

Tangerines
Bouletes de Saucisson*
Go-For-It Cheese Grits
Figue Gateau*
Creole-Dripped Coffee

Lunch

Opelousas Baked Chicken Legs*
Wheat Crackers • Cream Cheese •   Hot Pepper Jelly
Dried Honeyed Pineapple • Roasted Pecans
Julia's Camping Cookies* • Hot Coffee

Dinner

Oyster Cocktails*
Roast Sirloin Tip*
Shrimp Jambalaya in Pepper Shells*
Butter Rolls . Spiced Peaches*
Bon Temps Bread Pudding*
Campfire Brulot*
Wine: A smoky red like Kendall-Jackson Cabernet Sauvignon will do wonders for your Mardi Gras mambo.

Boulettes de Saucisson

An old Creole breakfast favorite, simplicity itself to heat and serve.

1 1/2 pounds ground pork
1 large clove garlic, minced
3/4 teaspoon cayenne
1 1/2 teaspoons salt
  or to taste
3/4 teaspoon sage
1 small onion, grated
  in two batches
2 tablespoons minced parsley

Flour to dredge meat balls
Oil to cover skillet 1/4-inch
  deep
4 tablespoons flour
1 cup water
1 cup milk
Salt and pepper to taste
2 tablespoons minced parsley
  to garnish

At Home: Mix pork and seasonings, including half the grated onion. Form into plum-sized balls, dredge in flour and fry in hot oil until golden brown. Remove boulettes, pour off oil and return 4 tablespoons oil to pan. Sprinkle oil with 4 tablespoons flour and brown lightly. Add water, milk, half the grated onion, and the boulettes and simmer 20 minutes. Salt and pepper to taste and sprinkle with minced parsley. Transport in Ziploc freezer bag or plastic container.

In Camp: Heat gently with more milk, if necessary. Serve over Go-For-It Cheese Grits. Makes 6 servings (about 30 boulettes).

Figue Gateau

Creole fig cake, a quickly made, quick-to-disappear coffeecake or simple dessert.

1 cup sugar
2 eggs, beaten
1/2 cup oil
2 cups all-purpose flour
1 1/2 teaspoons baking soda
1 teaspoon salt

1 teaspoon cinnamon
1/2 teaspoon allspice
1 teaspoon vanilla
1 cup fig preserves
1 cup chopped pecans

At Home: Stir together sugar, eggs, and oil. Mix in flour, baking soda, salt, cinnamon, allspice, vanilla, fig preserves, and pecans. Bake in preheated 350-degree oven in buttered 10-inch iron skillet for about 30 minutes or until lightly browned and tests done. Let cool slightly and turn out in cake tin.

To Pack: Cake.

In Camp: Serve warm. Makes 8 servings.

Opelousas Baked Chicken Legs

Five minutes of your time rewards you with a meltingly tender and spicy entree. Good for duck, too. Served with Dirty Rice and J.D.'s Yams, either makes a South Louisiana dinner par excellence.

1 teaspoon salt or to taste
1 teaspoon pepper
2 teaspoons paprika
1 teaspoon chili powder
1 teaspoon garlic salt

1 teaspoon cayenne or to taste
12 chicken legs,
   skinned if you like
Water
Oil

At Home: Combine seasonings and coat chicken. Arrange chicken in large baking pan in single layer, drizzle with small amount oil if chicken is not fat and just cover the bottom of the pan with water. Bake at 275 dgreees for 2 hours or until chicken is very tender, turning once. Baste frequently. Transport in Zip-loc freezer bag.

To Pack: Chicken.

In Camp: Serve hot (steamed) or cold.

Julia's Camping Cookies

Like Julia, you don't have to camp to love these cookies.

2 cups all-purpose flour
1 teaspoon baking powder
1 teaspoon salt
3/4 teaspoon baking soda
1 cup margarine
2 cups brown sugar
2 eggs

1 tablespoon water
1 1/2 teaspoons grated
   orange rind
1 1/2 cups granola
1 (6-ounce) package semi-
   sweet chocolate chips
1/2 cups nuts, chopped

At Home: Combine flour, baking powder, salt, and baking soda. Cream brown sugar and margarine; add eggs and beat till light. Add water and rind. Add flour mixture and mix well. Stir in remaining ingredients. Drop by tablespoonfuls 3 inches apart on cookie sheet. Bake at 375 degrees for 12 minutes or until lightly browned. Makes 3 dozen. Transport in oatmeal box or Ziploc bag.

To Pack: Cookies.

In Camp: Serve with coffee.

Oyster Cocktails

Simple and impressive as the very dickens served in camp where folks least expect to find them.

Shucked raw oysters　　　　Lettuce
Cocktail Sauce　　　　　　Lemon wedges

At Home: Make sauce and transport in jar. Wash and dry lettuce and transport in Ziploc bag.

To Pack: Oysters in disposable plastic or glass jar, lettuce, sauce, lemon, small tongs, styrofoam cups.

In Camp: Set out oysters and tongs to serve them, along with cocktail sauce and a pile of shredded lettuce and lemon wedges. Let each oyster fan concoct a cocktail in a styrofoam cup—inelegant but disposable.

Roast Sirloin Tip

Low temperature roasting insures a tender, succulent roast.

1 (4-pound) sirloin tip roast　　Freshly-ground pepper
Slivered garlic cloves　　　　　Cayenne
Vegetable oil

At Home: Make slits in roast and insert garlic slivers. Rub roast with oil, set it on rack in preheated 275-degree oven with a meat thermometer inserted in thickest part. Roast until thermometer reaches 140 degrees. Remove immediately. Cool roast and transport it and juices in Ziploc freezer bag.

To Pack: Roast, freshly-ground pepper, salt, sharp knife.

In Camp: Slowly heat roast and juices in actual or improvised (from nesting pots) double boiler or wrap roast in heavy foil and heat over grill. This slow heating takes a while, but fast heating toughens the meat, so start early. Once roast is *gently* heated through, slice, and season with salt and freshly-ground pepper. (you may need to add a bit of water to double boiler.) Serves 8.

Shrimp Jambalaya in Pepper Shells

Serve this deeply spicy jambalaya without the pepper shells, if you prefer.

1 1/4 cups white rice, cooked
1/2 cup finely chopped green pepper
1/2 cup finely chopped celery
1 cup finely chopped onion
1 teaspoon minced garlic
1/4 teaspoon cayenne or to taste
1/2 teaspoon oregano
1 bay leaf

1/4 teaspoon paprika
1/4 teaspoon white pepper
1/2 teaspoon pepper
3/4 teaspoon salt
1/2 teaspoon thyme
2 tablespoons bacon fat or oil
1 cup chopped tomatoes
1 cup chicken or shrimp stock (or more, if necessary)
2 cups peeled fresh shrimp
6 medium green peppers

At Home: Cook rice and set aside. Chop vegetables and set aside. Combine seasonings and set aside. In large deep skillet, saute vegetables in fat or oil until onions are clear. Add tomatoes, stock, and seasonings, and simmer very gently 1/2 hour, adding more liquid if necessary to keep it moist. Add shrimp and simmer just till shrimp turn pink, then combine rice with other ingredients, adding more stock if mixture seems dry. Correct seasoning. Cut tops off peppers and steam or boil till just tender, about 12 minutes. Drain and fill with jambalaya. Wrap peppers individually in foil.

To Pack: Stuffed peppers, steamer, tongs.

In Camp: Heat foil-wrapped peppers in top of steamer. Makes enough for 6 medium peppers or 4-6 servings.

Spiced Peaches

Country folk haved a weakness for these. Bet you will, too.

1 (1-pound 13-ounce) can freestone peaches	1 teaspoon whole cloves
1/4 cup raspberry vinegar	1 teaspoon allspice
	1 teaspoon peppercorns

At Home: Pour peach syrup in saucepan. Add vinegar, cloves, allspice, and peppercorns and bring to boil. Pour over peaches in large widemouth jar or plastic container. Makes about 8 peach halves.

To Pack: Peaches.

In Camp: Serve as a relish with bland or spicy food.

Bon Temps Bread Pudding

New Orleans' best is naturally the world's best. (If you think we're chauvinistic, start cooking and judge for yourself.)

5 cups milk	1 teaspoon cinnamon
6 tablespoons butter	1 teaspoon vanilla (for exqui-
3/4 cup golden raisins	site vanilla at dirt cheap
5 large eggs	prices, buy it in Mexico)
2 cups sugar	15 cups stale French bread
1 teaspoon nutmeg	cubes (about 2 large loaves)

At Home: Melt butter in milk. Cover raisins with hot water for 5 minutes and drain. Whisk eggs, sugar, spices, and vanilla. Gradually add milk, whisking. Add raisins and bread. Place in 2 buttered bread pans and place them in larger pan filled halfway with hot water. Bake at 350 degrees until top is browned and knife inserted in center comes out clean (50 minutes to 1 hour).

MARIAPAZ'S WHISKEY SAUCE

| 1/2 pound brown sugar | 1/2 stick butter |
| 2 ounces good bourbon | 1/2 cup heavy cream |

At Home: Place ingredients in saucepan and simmer until slightly thickened, whisking occasionally. Do not overcook or sauce will harden. Pour sauce over top of bread pudding in bread pan and wrap well in heavy foil. Or carry sauce in jar to reheat over Sterno canned heat. Makes 1 1/2 cups.

To Pack: Bread pudding, sauce, and Sterno.

In Camp: Warm pudding over boiling water. Serves 10-12.

Campfire Brulot

Just a taste is all you need, but what a taste!

1/2 cup sugar	Peel of 1/2 small orange
1/2 cup good bourbon	Peel of 1/2 small lemon
15 whole cloves	3 cups hot dark roast coffee
1 (2-inch) stick cinnamon	

At Home: Mix sugar, bourbon, spices, and peel, and transport in jar.

To Pack: Bourbon mixture, pre-made coffee, drip coffeepot bottom.

In Camp: Place bourbon mixture in bottom of drip coffeepot and heat. Just before it boils, remove from heat and light with match. After alcohol is burned off, add hot coffee and serve at once. (If you don't bring the coffeepot bottom, bring a strainer.) Makes 6 small servings.

6

Cross-Country Skiing
from a Carolina Condo:
A North Carolina Ski Outing

You can't really call it camping, what with the microwave, the double oven, and the jacuzzi, but for some of us, a winter condominium ski trip comes close. The big difference is that we're camping out in someone else's tax shelter instead of under a sweet gum tree. Granted, we don't cook on a camp stove, but since a winter skiing getaway sets us back a month or two on the rent money, we do haul our meals in ice chests, cutting costs and condo KP duty at the same time. And because cross-country skiing is practically the most strenuous activity known to man, condo-campers have every right to grand food and lots of it.

Last year we and our ice chests hit our poorman's condo just right. The night we arrived in Asheville, a surprise snow filled the North Carolina woods so deep that next morning we simply skied out the back door and up onto the Blue Ridge Parkway just a few minutes away.

The Parkway in winter, closed to motor traffic, belongs to cross-country skiers. High above the city in the silent crystal air, we shushed along on a trail broken by only a few early morning skiers. Every once in a while we'd break out of the snow-iced Christmas trees lining our trail into a skywide panorama of mountains stretching blue-white and endless. If my sister Laurie's roast capon dinner hadn't lured us home, we'd have skied ourselves all the way to Mount Pisgah.

For information on North Carolina skiing:

Diamond Brand Camping
  Center
Highway 25
Naples, NC 28760
704/684-6262

Blue Ridge Parkway
  National Park Service
700 Northwestern Plaza
Asheville, NC 28801
704/259-0779

National Forests in North Carolina
P. O. Box 2750
Asheville, NC 28802
704/257-4200

Brochures and maps sent on
on request

Heading for the Blue Ridge Parkway, cross-counrty skiers break an early morning trail.

MENUS

(*indicates recipes given)

Breakfast

Apricot Nectar • Carolina Scrapple*
Rich Apple Compote with Cream* • Coffee

Lunch

Van Holten's Creole Reuben Sandwiches*
Rib-Sticking Pea Soup*
Rich Camp Hot Cocoa • Walker's Imported Shortbread

Dinner

Chopped Liver and French Bread*
Roast Capon with Blackberry Sauce* • Ginger Carrots*
Pecan Rice* • Bleu Cheese Romaine Salad*
Mona's Sweet Potato Soul Pie*
Wine: A boxom white like Rodney Strong Chardonnay

Carolina Scrapple

If you've never tasted scrapple, what are you waiting for? It's one of the original "comfort foods."

1 pound boneless pork	1/2 teaspoon sage
(or 1 1/2 pounds with bones)	1/4 teaspoon garlic powder
Water	Chicken bouillon cubes
1 teaspoon salt	1 1/4 cups yellow corn meal
1/2 teaspoon pepper	1/2 cup onion, chopped

At Home: Cook meat in water seasoned with salt, pepper, sage, and garlic powder until very tender. Remove meat from broth and chop. Measure broth. Either reduce it to 6 cups or add water and chicken bouillon cubes at a rate of 1 cube to 1 cup to equal 6 cups. Stir in cornmeal and cook until thick, about 20 minutes, stirring occasionally. (Don't scorch it!) Stir in chopped meat and onion and check seasoning. Pour into loaf pan and chill. Transport in pan tightly wrapped in heavy foil.

To Pack: Scrapple, fat or shortening.

In Condo or Camp: Slice scrapple and fry in hot fat until hot and browned. Serves 8.

Rich Apple Compote with Cream

6 large firm apples
Brown sugar to taste
1/2 cup water
1/4 teaspoon nutmeg

1 stick cinnamon
1/4 teaspoon allspice
Grated rind of 1/2 orange

At Home: Pare, core, and quarter apples. Put in saucepan with brown sugar, water, spices, and rind and simmer gently, covered, until they form a rich, tender compote. Transport in plastic container.

To Pack: Compote, heavy cream.

In Condo or Camp: Serve warm with cream. This is also a good simple dessert. Serves 3-4.

Van Holten's Creole Reuben Sandwiches

These zingy sandwiches are good hot or cold, but they are only as good as what goes in them, so buy the best: your own corned beef, simmered or oven-roasted; imported Swiss cheese; and Van Holten's cold-pack sauerkraut from the dairy case. (Are Jerry and Ruth Van Holten my uncle and aunt? Never mind, I'd recommend their delicious sauerkraut and pickles even if they weren't.)

Fresh rye bread
Mayonnaise
Creole mustard
1/4 pound corned beef,
  sliced paper thin
1/8 pound imported Swiss
  cheese, sliced paper thin

1/4 cup Van Holten's
  sauerkraut, well-drained
  (drain in a colander and
  again on paper towels)

In Condo or Camp: Spread bread with mayonnaise and Creole mustard. Layer with corned beef, Swiss cheese, and Van Holten's sauerkraut. If sandwiches are to be served cold, wrap in heavy foil. If they are to be served warm, grill on greased griddle until cheese melts. Then wrap in heavy foil and place in insulated container to keep warm. Makes 1 sandwich.

Rib-Sticking Pea Soup

Serve this North country favorite on high-stress trips: skiing, winter hiking, cold-weather canoeing.

1 pound split peas
8 cups water
1 large onion, chopped
2 stalks celery, chopped
2 carrots, sliced
2 bay leaves
1 teaspoon thyme

1 1/2 teaspoons minced garlic
Meaty ham bone or
  1 1/2 cups diced ham
Salt and pepper to taste
1 large potato, diced
  (optional)

At Home: Simmer all ingredients until peas are soft. If hambone is used, remove and dice meat small. Freeze, if you like.

In Condo or Camp: Heat piping hot and serve. If you take it out for lunch, heat it to boiling and carry in widemouth thermos. Serves 4-6.

Chopped Liver with French Bread

The flavor of this spread is beyond good.

1/2 cup rendered chicken fat
(available in jars) or butter
2 small onions, minced

1 pound chicken livers
2 large eggs, hardboiled
Salt and pepper

At Home: Saute onion in fat until golden. Add livers and saute 2-3 minutes until brown outside and pink inside. Chop fairly small with eggs; season and chill overnight. Transport in plastic container. Makes 2 cups.

In Condo or Camp: Serve on thin-sliced French bread. This also makes a mean sandwich on rye bread with lettuce and onion.

Roast Capon with Blackberry Sauce

Delicately raised, I only recently learned what a capon was. I regret the wasted years.

1 capon, 7 pounds or so
Butter for basting

Salt and pepper

At Home or In Condo: Preheat oven to 300 degrees. Wash and dry capon. Remove giblets and boil for stock. Rub capon inside and out with butter and place on rack (above drippings that may accumulate) to roast. Insert meat thermometer in thickest part of thigh. Baste every half hour with butter and drippings and roast about 35-45 minutes per pound or until thermometer reads 185 degrees. Remove from oven and salt and pepper capon.

BLACKBERRY SAUCE

1/2 cup butter
1 cup sugar
2 cups raspberry or other
  mild vinegar
2 cups fresh or unsweetened
  frozen, thawed blackberries

1/4 cup Chambord (black
  raspberry liqueur—you
  can substitute brandy)
1/2 cup chicken stock

At Home: Melt butter. Add sugar and cook till light brown, stirring occasionally. Gradually stir in vinegar and blackberries and boil till reduced to about 1 1/2 cups, stirring occasionally—about 15-20 minutes. Add Chambord or brandy and bring to boil. Add 1/2 cup stock and simmer 5 minutes. Makes about 4 cups.

To Pack: Capon, Blackberry Sauce.

In Condo or Camp: Serve capon freshly-roasted (or carved and reheated in large pot) with hot Blackberry Sauce. Plan on using leftovers for sandwiches. Serves 8.

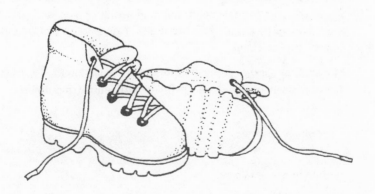

Ginger Carrots

4 tablespoons butter
1/4 cup brown sugar
1 1/2 teaspoons ginger (powdered or fresh and chopped)

1 pound baby carrots, peeled,
sliced julienne, and
boiled just tender

At Home or In Condo: Melt butter. Add sugar and ginger and cook 3 minutes. Add carrots and simmer 5 minutes to glaze.

To Pack: Carrots.

In Condo or Camp: Reheat carrots. Serves 4.

Pecan Rice

Suave yet nutty, this Cary Grant of rice dishes suits just about anyone.

2 cups rice, cooked
1/2 cup butter

1/2 cup finely chopped pecans
Minced parsley for garnish

At Home: Saute pecans in butter until browned but not burned. Toss pecans and butter with hot cooked rice, and garnish with minced parsley. Makes 6 cups.

To Pack: Rice.

In Condo or Camp: Reheat rice with a little water.

Bleu Cheese Romaine Salad

1 large crisp head romaine
1/4 pound bleu cheese
1/4 cup minced ripe olives
1 cup olive oil

1/3 tarragon vinegar
3 slices bacon, cooked
crisp and crumbled

At Home: Wash and trim romaine and transport in Ziploc bag. Make dressing by combining bleu cheese, olives, olive oil, and vinegar. Fry bacon and transport in Ziploc bag.

To Pack: Romaine, dressing, bacon.

In Condo or Camp: Dry romaine thoroughly, tear into bite-size pieces, toss with enough dressing just to coat leaves, and sprinkle with bacon. Serves 6-8.

Mona's Sweet Potato Soul Pie

This humble-sounding pie tastes real uptown.

2 cups cooked mashed sweet
   potatos
1 cup packed brown sugar
1/2 cup margarine, softened
2 eggs, separated
1/2 teaspoon ginger

1/2 teaspoon cinnamon
1/2 teaspoon nutmeg
1/2 cup evaporated milk
1/4 cup sugar
1 unbaked (10-inch) pie shell
Whipped cream (optional)

At Home: Combine sweet potatoes, brown sugar, margarine, egg yolks, spices, and evaporated milk and beat till light. Beat egg whites foamy, gradually add sugar, beating until stiff. Fold into potato mixture. Spoon into shell and bake at 400 degrees for 10 minutes. Reduce heat to 350 degrees and bake 40 minutes or until set. Wrap in heavy foil and keep cool.

To Pack: Pie, heavy cream.

In Condo or Camp: Warm pie and serve with whipped cream or plain. Makes 6-8 servings.

A pause for a picture to recapture the memories.

A Select List of Recommended Reading

Alabama Canoe Rides and Floats
John Foshee
Strode Publishers, Inc.
Reliable information on Alabama rivers.

The Art of Eating
M.F.K. Fisher
Random House
Food for the table, food for the mind.

Bicycling in the Back Roads of French Louisiana
Dr. and Mrs. Richard Williams
Lafayette Natural History Museum and Planetarium
637 Girard Park Drive
Lafayette, LA 70503
Grand bicycling in the Bayou State.

Billy Joe Tatum's Wild Foods Cookbook & Field Guide
Workman Publishing Company
Good hunting, good cooking.

Canoeing in Louisiana
Dr. and Mrs. Richard Williams
Lafayette Natural History Museum and Planetarium
637 Girard Park Drive
Lafayette, LA 70503
Necessary for plotting all Louisiana paddles.

The Complete Wilderness Paddler
James West Davidson and John Rugge
Alford A. Knopf
Planning, outfitting, and conducting the ultimate canoe odyssey.

The Explorers Ltd. Source Book
Compiled and written by Explorers Ltd.
Harper & Row
Maps, services, gear suppliers and sources.

A Field Guide to Edible Wild Plants of Eastern/Central North America
Lee Allen Peterson
Houghton-Mifflin Company
Excellent for plant identification.

The Maine Atlas and Gazetteer
DeLorme Publishing Co.
All you need to know about camping in Maine.

Stalking the Wild Asparagus
Stalking the Healthful Herbs
Euell Gibbons
David McKay Company, Inc.
The granddaddy of all weedeaters.

Trail Guide to the Delta Country
New Orleans Group of the Sierra Club
Canoeing, cycling, hiking, biking in the Louisiana/Mississippi Delta. Check local map and people for updates on such things as safe places for shuttle cars.

Vagabonding in America
Ed Buryn
Random House
How to travel in America: camping, car camping, bicycling, hiking, backpacking, medical information.

Index

About the Author

Joan Wilcox Osborne

Born in Milwaukee, Wisconsin, Joan's family moved to Louisiana when she was only four, and except for a two-year taste of the Florida beaches, has lived in Louisiana every since. She holds an M.S. in Zoology and an M.A. in Counseling from Louisiana State University, and has worked as a biologist, counselor, and outdoor guide.

Joan Osborne has led hundreds of camping trips for the Sierra Club, Wilderness Adventurers, and for private clients. She has published numerous articles on camping for newspapers and magazines. She enjoys all of the challenges of the outdoors—but by her own admission, "I always stack the deck and bring along good food for a reward. To me the good life will always be better outdoors, as long as I'm accompanied by good companions and good food."

Joan is married to Tim Fields and has two children, Johnny and Caroline.

"Best of the Best" Cookbook Series:

Best of the Best from Mississippi $12.95   0-937552-09-7
Best of the Best from Tennessee $ 12.95   0-937552-20-8
Best of the Best from Florida $12.95   0-937552-16-X
Best of the Best from Louisiana $12.95   0-937552-13-5
Best of the Best from Kentucky $12.95   0-937552-27-5
Best of the Best from Alabama $12.95   0-937552-28-3
Best of the Best from Texas $14.95   0-937552-14-3

The Quail Ridge Press Cookbook Series:

The Little Gumbo Book $6.95   0-937552-17-8
Gourmet Camping $10.95   0-937552-23-2
Hors D'Oeuvres Everybody Loves $5.95   0-937552-11-9
The Seven Chocolate Sins $5.95   0-937552-01-1
A Salad A Day $5.95   0-937552-02-X
Quickies for Singles $5.95   0-937552-03-8
Twelve Days of Christmas Cookbook $5.95   0-937552-00-3
The Country Mouse Cheese Cookbook $5.95   0-937552-10-0

Send check, money order, or VISA/MasterCard number with expiration date to:

QUAIL RIDGE PRESS
P.O. Box 123
Brandon, MS 39043

Please add $1.50 postage and handling.
Gift wrap with enclosed card add $1.00.
Mississippi residents add 6% sales tax.
Phone orders call: 601/825-2063.